A MUSICAL PILGRIMAGE

By
NICK ROSSI

BOSTON
BRANDEN PRESS
PUBLISHERS

In memory of my good friend and mentor, the late
MARIO CASTELNUOVO-TEDESCO
(1895– 1968)

PREFACE

By academic training I am a musicologist. By profession – a music educator. By avocation – a traveler, amateur photographer, an avid reader. These interests and activities led me to undertake a most unusual and unique project, the end result of which is *A Musical Pilgrimage*, an account of this author's fascinating, often intriguing excursions to Europe with a friend – another amateur photographer – trying to retrace the steps of the immortal masters of music.

The pilgrimage started with a visit to the little thatch-roofed cottage in Rohrau, lower Austria, in which Josef Haydn was born in 1732, and led through countless homes, schools and churches to conservatories, concert halls and opera houses. Our travels took us not only to European countries, but behind the Iron Curtain to Hungary (from which we almost didn't "escape"), to Czechoslovakia (before the invasion of late-1968), and to East Germany (where Russian soldiers on leave took photographs of us to send to their families back home to show them what "Westerners" really look like). The trip ended with a pleasant afternoon spent at *Le Belvédère*, the little home about 50 km from Paris which Maurice Ravel purchased in 1920 and in which he lived up to the time of his death in 1937.

In the course of our travels I had the thrill of playing on Schubert's favorite piano in the parlor of the apartment in which he was born. I climbed the rickety stairs in the parish church of Le Roncole to the loft where Giuseppe Verdi – as a lad of five – had gone to practise the pipe organ, the same one on which I now had the thrill of playing. We even discovered the house in which Mozart composed his three greatest symphonies, a building which, according to the Viennese authorities, had long since been razed!

3

The author would like to express his thanks and gratitude to a number of people who were of great assistance in this musical pilgrimage. This group would include the directors of the Beethovenhaus in Bonn, the Mozarteum in Salzburg, and the Scala Museum in Milan. Also to be thanked are biographers who gave generously of their time in correspondence with me: the noted Haydn scholar, Dr. Karl Geiringer; the Verdi biographer, George R. Marek; and the English man of letters and authority on Claude Debussy, Edward Lockspeiser. For the privilege of visiting Sant'Agata and Torre del Lago, this author wishes to convey his appreciation to Dr. Alberto Carrara Verdi and his wife, and to Signora Rita Puccini, respectively.

It is this author's hope that the pages of *A Musical Pilgrimage* provide a few moments of pleasure for the reader, whether he be a "fan" of music or a practising musician.

NICK ROSSI

Sacramento, California

4

CONTENTS

Place of Count Harrach for whom Mathias Haydn worked as a wheelwright. It was here that Mathias first met his future wife who at that time worked as one of the cooks in the palace.

Thatched-roofed cottage in the village of Rohrau built by Mathias Haydn for his new bride. It was here that their son Josef was born on March 31, 1732.

I
HAYDN, THE WORLD'S MOST HONORED SERVANT

There is a broad, bustling highway which heads southeast out of neon-lit downtown Vienna with its gaudy "Coca-Cola" and "Fly Now – Pay Later" signs plastered against eighteenth-century facades. As one battles streetcars, trucks and impatient autoists along this busy roadway, one first passes the sprawling city cemetery with its reminders of the past; then the road follows on toward the *flughafen* – the airport to the future.

Once beyond these vestiges of the twentieth century, the roadway narrows and wanders through verdant fields of corn and grass, passing over narrow little bridges across meandering streams. Traffic becomes sparse except for an occasional horse-drawn haywagon; it's as though time were being turned back a hundred, perhaps two hundred years.

Driving by an old castle partially hidden by a lush growth of trees and shrubs and surrounded by an old wall, I remarked to our guide – a graduate music student from the University of Vienna – about the view I glimpsed through the archway. He told me that this was the ancestral home of the Harrachs. And then it all came back to me: I had stumbled accidentally on the chronological beginning of our pilgrimage. It had been for Count Harrach that Mathias Haydn worked, making wheels for his coaches and repairing wagons. It was in this very building that Mathias met a young servant girl, a cook, and fell in love with her. Soon they were married.

In the quaint little village of Rohrau, only a few miles away from Count Harrach's estate, Mathias Haydn built a home for his new bride, a small but handsome building with whitewashed walls and a thatched roof. Although it burned to the ground a century later, it was authentically rebuilt because it was the house in which their son, the composer Franz Josef Haydn, was born on March 31, 1732.

7

As we drove through Rohrau — a "one-street" village — I spotted the Haydn home immediately, for it is the only remaining one with a thatched roof. My romantic imagination had already turned back the clock: I saw the old artisan at work on a carriage as young Josef played in the central courtyard. I was rudely awakened from my reverie, though, for there in front of the main entrance was a bulldozer and a scoop shovel digging a trough for a new sewer main! The workmen were very nice, however, and moved their vehicles so that some pictures could be taken without this twentieth-century incongruity. The biggest problem was with the neighborhood children, all of whom were interested in this new hole in the ground and wanted to pose for pictures beside it.

The building looks much as it appears in eighteenth-century engravings: a wide, single-story structure with a heavy thatched roof. The green window frames stand out boldly against the white walls. A little flower bed of bright blossoms is enclosed behind a green picket fence which separates it from the roadway.

In typical European fashion, the home is built around a central courtyard where one rested from a hard day's labor, kept the chickens, and harnessed the horses. The furniture has, of course, disappeared from the rooms, but a few period pieces — of the type an artisan would have made — are scattered about. The building now serves as a Haydn museum, with contemporary etchings as well as copies of paintings on display. What is left of a statue that Count Harrach had erected on his estate to honor Haydn's sixtieth birthday may be seen, looking now more like a marble bust than the full size statue that it once was.

THE EDUCATION OF JOSEPH HAYDN

We drove over another narrow road, first crossing the flatlands around Rohrau and then climbing into some rolling hills. As we approached the Danube river about eight miles away, the town of Hainburg (or Haimburg as it appears on old

8

maps) came into view. We drove through the "Vienna City" gate, a portal in the old Roman wall that once completely surrounded the village. Close by we saw an ivy-covered house of stone and mortar, the home of Haydn's paternal grandmother.

As a lad of six, Haydn made the journey to Hainburg to live and study with his cousin Johann. The old church of St. Josef and St. John is still the center of the town, its towers rising above the red-slate roofs and chimney pots of the village shops and houses. It was here that cousin Johann directed the singers and instrumentalists for every service, looked after the church clock, rang the bells for special occasions and emergencies such as thunderstorms and fires. In addition, he instructed eighty children, including Josef, in reading, writing, arithmetic, singing, and prayers.

From Hainburg the country road leads south about thirty-eight miles to Eisenstadt where Haydn was employed by the Counts Esterházy for more than forty years. But we are getting ahead of our story. From Hainburg Haydn went to Vienna to sing in the choir of St. Stephen's Cathedral; the cathedral looks as imposing today as it must have appeared to the boy of eight. With its high, vaulted ceiling and impressive central nave, the choir loft where Josef sang and where he studied organ can still be seen , although the organ — for practical reasons — has been rebuilt.

The modern visitor to Vienna may visit some of the impressive spots where Haydn sang with the "Vienna Choir Boys." Schönbrunn Palace — which was then still under construction — remains one of the great show places of Europe and is but a few miles from the cathedral. With magnificent galleries and regal apartments, the contrast can be imagined between the drab choir school in which Haydn lived and this opulent example of rococo decor. Just past the Kahlenburg — the Vienna woods — is Klosterneuberg, a monastery where Haydn, no longer a soprano, made one of his final appearances before he was forced to leave the choir.

Thrown out into the world, his only possessions were, as he later wrote, "three ragged shirts and a worn coat." He moved into an attic apartment with a friend, an old building which can still be seen through the Imperial Gates of the Palace in central Vienna.

There is a charming little turreted castle about thirty miles northwest of Vienna which belonged in those days to Count Furnberg, one of Haydn's first patrons. Having met Haydn at a summer resort where the composer had gone as a valet to his music teacher, Nicolo Porpora, the Count invited Haydn to stay at his country home and play with his orchestra. A plaque on the front of the old building — now the Weinzierl School — reminds one that it was here that Haydn wrote some of his very first quartets and symphonies.

HAYDN AND THE ESTERHAZYS

There are two principal castles with which Haydn was associated for most of his adult life. One was the ancestoral residence of the Esterházy family at Eisenstadt in Austria, about thirty miles southeast of Vienna. The other castle was built at Fertöd in Hungary during Haydn's lifetime.

As we approached Eisenstadt, the castle was clearly visible, perched on a little knoll overlooking the town. Although the town itself has increased in size since the days of Haydn, the exterior of the castle looks just as it does in eighteenth-century paintings. Once we had parked the car and walked inside, changes were obvious. What once had been a sumptuous residence was now, in effect, the town hall, with countless offices partitioned out of former suites of rooms. Where once Prince Paul Esterházy had ruled his vast holdings of twenty-one castles, sixty market towns, two hundred dairy farms, and four hundred villages from this enormous castle, Dr. Paul Esterházy now "administers" the region around Eisenstadt as a mayor from his office on the ground floor.

One gallery has been preserved, though — the Music Salon where Haydn and his orchestra used to perform almost nightly. It is a high-ceilinged room with tall, narrow windows. The walls

10

Parish church in Hainburg where Josef Haydn's cousin Johann served as organist. As a boy Josef received his first singing and pipe organ lessons in the loft of this church from his cousin.

Weinzierl, now a school, formerly the Castle of Count Fürnburg who was one of Haydn's first patrons. It was for performance at this estate that Haydn composed his first twelve string quartets.

are white with gold Baroque decor embossed from floor to ceiling. Countless oil frescos, done with infinite care and fine detail, abound on the walls and ceiling. One is overwhelmed by the effect.

Although it is not always open to the public, the little private chapel of the castle is just down the hallway. The pipe organ in the Baroque chapel has been replaced, but the old console on which Haydn regularly played may be seen in a little anteroom before entering the chapel.

Diagonally across the street from the castle is the Burgkirche, the parish church, where many of Haydn's Masses were first performed and where he is now buried. About two blocks down the street is the little home that the Prince provided for Haydn and his wife. It is a small two-story house built around a little courtyard. Today this home is another of the Haydn museums. A couple of his harpsichords are on display; a hidden phonograph plays one of his sonatas softly in the background. There are a few pieces of furniture remaining, the shelves of one breakfront filled with gifts and tokens of gratitude bestowed on Haydn during his lifetime by the reigning royalty of more than half-a-dozen countries.

ESTERHÁZA

The other principal Esterházy castle is in Hungary, near the city of Soparön in Fertöd. This is the famous Esterháza (literally, the "home" of the "Esterházy's"), built during Haydn's lifetime on the Neuseidlersee by Prince Nicholas at a cost in excess of five million dollars. It fell into disrepair during the years following World War I, and was used first by the Germans and then by the Russians as an army barracks during World War II. It was sacked, the walls defaced, and the floors heavily gouged.

Under the communist regime of Hungary, millions of dollars have been spent in the last few years trying to restore it, not to commemorate the Esterházys but to honor their servant, Josef Haydn. It is no longer called Esterháza, but the Fertöd Castle. It

12

Grand ballroom with ornate Baroque ceiling in the Esterházy Castle
at Eisenstadt. For more than forty years Haydn conducted his new
symphonies and concertos in this salon.

Parlor of Haydn's home in Eisenstadt, provided by Count Nicholas
Esterházy. Many of Haydn's compositions for the court were first
played here in the quiet of his own home.

13

is open to the public, and most of the rooms in the main wing have been well restored. The furnishings are sparse, and in place of the fabulous collection of paintings that once enhanced the walls, a rather sad collection of tired tapestries now hang. The grounds are once again beautifully landscaped.

Getting there is half the problem, though. To procure a visa we had to spend almost half a day at the Hungarian embassy in Vienna, waiting in line, being interviewed, and having innumerable papers processed. (We made no attempt to take our Austrian student guide with us.)

Once armed with these papers we headed for the Hungarian border about thirty miles southeast of Eisenstadt. As we approached the control point, the pair of parallel high barbed-wire fences were very much in evidence. Watch towers appeared at regular intervals, manned by soldiers with machine guns "at the ready." Land mines and tank barriers cover the distance between the two parallel fences. With passports and visas we had no trouble getting into Hungary, although we were stopped at control points every five kilometers to check over our papers again.

Passing through Soparön, a city of good size, we felt for the first time the austerity of life in communist Hungary. There were almost no cars on the broad cobblestoned avenues; the few automobiles to be seen were of ancient vintage. The people walking on the sidewalks or sitting in the parks — for it was Sunday — were dressed in drab colors; no smiles were on their faces. Most of the visitors at the Castle had arrived by bicycle or on foot. One wonders what these folk must have thought as they looked at the opulence of this restoration and then had to return to their dreary existence under the severe strictures of the communist government.

Our return from Hungary to Austria was not as easy as our entry. As we learned later, our harassment at the border was part of a treatment frequently tendered visitors from the United States. We approached the control point and handed over our papers. After sitting patiently for thirty minutes, watching quite

Main entrance to Esterházy (now called by the Hungarians "Fertöd Castle") built during Haydn's lifetime by his patron Prince Nicholas Esterházy. Each year during Nicholas' reign the court moved here for part of the year.

Haydn statue in front of Mariahilfer Church on one of Vienna's busiest thoroughfares. This was Haydn's parish church in later life when he lived in retirement in Vienna.

15

a number of people of other nationalities cross easily back to Austria, I queried the Passport Officer about the delay. His English, which was quite good when we entered, was suddenly non-existent!

Finally after two hours of sitting in the car, waiting, our passports were returned to us. The Customs Officer checked under the seats, behind the door panels, and even looked inside the gasoline tank spigot. In suddenly excellent English he wished us "a good journey" and then we were on our way!

HAYDN'S VIENNA HOME

On a quiet residential street a few blocks from Vienna's main shopping district is Haydn's last home. It was this house that Haydn's wife encouraged him to buy after his journey to London; she wanted a place in which to live out her old age. After the composer purchased the building he added a second floor and developed its courtyard. In the music room of this home he composed *The Creation, The Seasons*, and his personal favorite, *The Austrian National Anthem*. The master claimed that most of his inspiration for these major works came while he was spending sunny hours relaxing in the courtyard.

Today this building is the only Haydn museum in Vienna; it is a sad and disappointing one. In no way does it recall the very talented, jovial, and warm individual who lived here. The rooms are cold and austere. The music room is painted a bright, almost Kelly green. Neither drapes adorn the windows nor a rug the floor. A lone harpsichord is the only piece of furniture in the room. The courtyard is even more bleak: one tree and three garbage cans were all that were to be seen. Except to know that this is the building in which Haydn spent his last years, it is hardly worth a visit.

Much more inspiring is a trip to the Mariahilfer Church in the busy shopping district a few blocks away. There in front of this beautiful Baroque church is a handsome statue of the master. The sculptor has captured both what we assume to be his

16

physical likeness and the benevolent yet witty spirit of the man. In beholding this monument to Franz Josef Haydn we recall the glory and splendor of eighteenth-century Vienna, the wonderful chamber music of the master, his wide variety of symphonies, and his mighty oratorios. We remember some words the master penned in one of his final letters.

"There are but a few contented and happy men here below; grief and care prevail everywhere; perhaps my labors may one day be the source from which the weary and worn, or the man burdened with affairs may derive a few moments rest."

Parlor of Mozart birthplace, Salzburg. In this room he received his first keyboard lessons from his father. An oil portrait of the lad when he was ten hangs on the wall above the instrument.

The "Pink Room" of Schönbrunn Palace, Vienna. When Mozart was six he performed for the Empress, Maria Theresa, and her court in this grand gallery of her newly erected Imperial Palace.

II
MOZART, A TALE OF MANY CITIES

Strange it is that the city which Mozart came to abhor — largely because of its tyrannical Archbishop — has been for the past few decades the focal point for homage to the composer with its annual Salzburg Festival!

This quaint old town at the foot of the great Alp mountains is situated on the Salzach River just after its dark and turbulent waters flow out of the Tyrols. It is dominated by the huge Hohensalzburg Fortress, the largest castle left intact in central Europe. This imposing structure, started in 1077, is located on the crest of a hill overlooking the entire Salzach valley, and as we climbed to its bastions we could see all of Salzburg before we wandered through its narrow, winding streets.

Dating from medieval times, the older part of Salzburg is located on the left bank of the river that bisects the city. As we strolled down one of its very small streets we came upon the six-storied structure in which Wolfgang Mozart was born on January 27, 1756. The building is now a fascinating museum. Entering from the street we saw the emblem of the Aesculap — the serpent in the lion's mouth — which was placed on the door by a chemist who purchased the building in 1585. The house changed ownership in 1703; the merchant who bought it from the chemist's descendents later rented some of its rooms to the newly married Leopold Mozart who had come from Augsburg to serve as a violinist at the Archbishop's court. Leopold's flat consisted of the bedroom in which his famous son as well as his daughter were born, a sitting room, a study, and a small reception room in which guests were received.

Like other houses of the Middle Ages, this one is narrow and deep; the back rooms of the building get their light from a small courtyard. At the head of the stairs we came upon the primitive kitchen which has been preserved as it was in Leopold's day, with ornate tiles over floors and walls, and with an old-fashioned open hearth for cooking. Across the hall the four rooms of his flat are now a museum which is well designed and reverently kept. Many well-known original portraits of Wolfgang Mozart and his family hang on the walls along with excellent copies of others. Documents, original manuscripts, memorabilia, and relics of the Mozart family abound, and the little violin on which the five-year-old Wolfgang learned to play without instruction rests in one of the showcases.

The most precious treasures in the collection are two Mozart keyboard instruments. The composer's piano, a *hammerflügel* constructed by Anton Walter in Vienna, was his favorite and the one he played in all the public performances of his last ten years. A clavichord was given to the museum by his widow Constance. Pasted in it is a note in her own handwriting: "On this instrument my husband Mozart composed, within five months, *The Magic Flute, The Clemency of Titus,* the *Requiem,* and a new freemason's cantata."

THE "DANCING MASTER'S HOUSE"

A short walk across the river brought us to the "Dancing Master's House" which faces the magnificent Mirabell Gardens. It was built at the beginning of the seventeenth century outside the medieval city walls and is spacious and full of windows, indicating the longing of this later period for space and light.

The house had been owned by a friend of Leopold Mozart's, a dancing instructor named Spöckner. On the latter's death in 1773, Leopold rented the home. His family occupied eight large, high-ceilinged rooms on the second floor. During the five and a half years Wolfgang lived here with his family, he created divertimenti, the *Haffner* serenade, sonatas, symphonies, piano concertos, and several masses.

After Leopold's death in 1787 the building was rented by a printer who installed noisy presses in the rooms once devoted to the sound of elegant music. In 1935 the Mozarteum succeeded

The Cathedral of Salzburg. Mozart was baptized in this church, and later some of his first sacred compositions were performed here. At twenty he was appointed to the Archbishop's court.

Main gallery of the Residenz, Salzburg. This formerly was the temporal palace of the Archbishop of Salzburg. Many of Mozart's first serenades, minuets, and divertimenti were written for performance in this room.

in renting the rooms formerly occupied by the Mozart family, and brought some of the old spirit of the house back to life. Unfortunately the building became the victim of the wartime bombing of 1944. In 1955 the Mozarteum purchased Leopold Mozart's music room and renovated it, restoring the decor to the correct style. Concerts are now held in this charming hall each year during the Salzburg Festival.

MOZART AND THE ARCHBISHOP

The medieval section of Salzburg centers around the Residenz, the temporal palace of the former Archbishops. The building, started in 1120 and redecorated in 1600, is majestic and impressive. Many of Mozart's minuets and serenades were first performed in its ornate galleries during the composer's appointment to the Archbishop's court. Today the Residenz is open to the public with frequent tours. As we wandered around its extensive royal apartments with ceiling frescos by Rottmayr and Altomonte, we could easily imagine the twenty-year-old Wolfgang appearing in dignified court dress to lead the musicians in one of his latest compositions.

Leaving the Residenz, we turned left and made the short walk to the Cathedral, the spiritual palace of the Archbishop. The Cathedral is an impressive and inspiring example of Italian late-Renaissance design. The cupola area, which was destroyed in a 1944 bomb attack, was well restored in 1959 to its original appearance. In this high-vaulted church dating from 1614 the young Wolfgang was baptized. Here, also, many of his masses were first performed.

Another church with which Mozart was associated (and in which Michael Haydn is buried) is two blocks away, St. Peter's Abbey Church. This is an older structure than the Cathedral, dating from 1130 and basically Romanesque in design.

Perhaps the most attractive of all the churches in this area is Mariaplain, a shrine about fifteen miles north of town on the Plainburg. It is a rustic version of the Cathedral; the interior is finished in the gaudiest and most detailed Baroque tradition. It

22

was late afternoon when we arrived and sunlight came streaming in the side windows, bouncing off the gold grill work of the main altar. The effect was enchanting for someone was practising the pipe organ softly. Mozart claimed that he frequently had a vision of this church as he traveled far away in foreign lands.

The Mozarteum in Salzburg is a specially designed building erected in 1910-1914 to house a permanent institution devoted to Mozart research and performance. In the pleasant little garden behind it we found "The Magic Flute Cottage."

When Mozart began work on *The Magic Flute* in the spring of 1791, he was already fatally ill. It may never be known whether this little cottage was a welcome retreat for him in his work, or whether the unscrupulous commissioner, librettist, and director of the Vienna Freihaustheater, Emanuel Schikaneder, had intended to keep Mozart in it under constraint to expedite work on the opera. At any rate, this frame bungalow was originally situated in one of the six open courtyards of the Freihaus in Vienna, and within its tiny, single room Mozart created *The Magic Flute* in barely five months.

After Mozart's death the cottage fell into disrepair and for a time was used by a poultry dealer to house his rabbits. When the Freihaus was put up for sale in 1873, the Mozart Foundation purchased the cottage and brought it to Salzburg. It was rebuilt in several different locations in Salzburg and was completely dismantled in 1948. It was then subjected to a thorough scientific process of preservation. In the summer of 1950 "The Magic Flute Cottage" was set up once more, this time in its present setting.

MOZART AND VIENNA

Although Mozart lived most of his adult life in Vienna, there is little left in this bustling modern city that recalls the spirit of the master. True, we visited the "Camesina House" where he composed most of *The Marriage of Figaro* and where Beethoven

23

and Haydn called on him, but these cold walls do little to remind one of the masters.

On the outskirts of Vienna is a little home — soon to be demolished — which in Mozart's day had the imposing name *Zu den drei Sternen*, "At the Three Stars." This was one of the composer's last dwellings, chosen because of its cheap rent, being at the time a considerable distance from town. It was here that Mozart completed the crowning achievement of his orchestral works, the last three symphonies.

In contrast to those humble dwellings, Vienna abounds in luxurious palaces in which Mozart performed as a child prodigy. Schönbrunn Palace, certainly the most regal and spacious of them, is now open to the public as a museum. As we toured through its salons and audience chambers we saw paintings of Maria Theresa's court gatherings, much like the ones for which Wolfgang performed.

In central Vienna most of the palaces Mozart knew — Count Kinsky's Palace, the Palais Collalto, and the Palace of Count Harrach — are now foreign embassies, and we could only observe the ancient facades of these buildings.

TRAVEL THROUGH COUNTLESS CITIES

Because Leopold Mozart booked his son on one concert tour after another from his fifth to twentieth year, it is almost impossible to visit a major European city that does not have some fond memories of the Mozart family and their visits. Old St. James' Palace in London was the scene of the triumphant appearance of Wolfgang and his sister Nannerl before King George III. In The Hague we viewed the Stadtholder's Court where the boy performed for Dutch royalty. He made a similar appearance at the Maison du Roi in Brussel's medieval town square. Paris was the highlight of the family's first major tour, and we visited the old Hôtel Bèauvais on the Rue François Miron where the Mozarts lived for several months with the Bavarian Minister of France. Versailles is a half-hour away by

Augsburg, birthplace of Mozart's father, and where Wolfgang bought his pianos.

The magic flute house, a small, one-room wooden structure built by Emanuel Schikaneder in the courtyard of his opera house so that Mozart could work in haste, undisturbed, setting Schikaneder's new libretto, *The Magic Flute*.

modern train, and we journeyed there to see its great gallery where eight-year-old Wolfgang played for King Louis XV.

Later tours took Mozart southward to Italy, and spots associated with the composer may still be visited in Milan, Naples, and Florence. We visited the beautiful palace and formal gardens of Count del Giardino in Verona where the Mozarts visited, and of course in Rome we stopped by the Sistine Chapel where Wolfgang first heard Allegri's *Miserere* and then rushed back to his lodgings to jot down a perfect copy from memory.

AUGSBURG AND PRAGUE

The two cities besides Salzburg that most suggest the spirit of Mozart are Augsburg in Germany and Prague in Czechoslovakia. These two cities do not necessarily have much in common, but somewhere within their history and tradition both have preserved the essence of their earlier years.

Most of the buildings on the main square in Augsburg date from the Middle Ages. We had written ahead for reservations at the Hotel Drei Mohren where we knew Leopold Mozart had stayed with his family two hundred years earlier. (He always booked them into the best hotel in town, assuming this would add stature to the family's appearance.) Unfortunately, the hotel was the only victim of wartime bombing on the main square and had been rebuilt in the late 1940's.

It was but a short walk from the hotel, however, to the home in which Leopold Mozart had been born. Today it is a museum and its rooms reconstructed to look as they did in former times.

Just a few doors down the street from the hotel is the old piano shop of Andreas Stein whose instruments fascinated young Mozart. "When Stein finishes one of these pianos," Wolfgang wrote home, "he sits down at it and trys all sorts of passages — runs, leaps and works away until the piano does simply everything."

Towards the end of his career Mozart and his wife became acquainted with the Dussek family whose Villa Bertramka was on the outer fringes of Prague. After the success of *The*

26

Central nave and altar of the Shrine of Mariaplain, about fifteen miles north of Salzburg on the Plainburg. It was Mozart's favorite church and the one for which he wrote his *Coronation Mass*.

Music room of Villa Bertramka, a room whose beauty caused Mozart to write home about its elegant decor. In all probability, much of *Don Giovanni* was first played over on this harpsichord.

Marriage of Figaro ("Nothing is played, sung or whistled in Prague but my Figaro," the composer wrote home) the Mozarts — already penniless and in grave financial straits — came to visit Bertramka. The composer often told his wife that those brief weeks in Prague were the happiest in his life and that he felt free from financial burdens and worries for the only time in his life.

We had no trouble in getting to Prague, for the Czechs were then courting tourist travel. As in all communist countries, we had to pay for all hotel rooms and meals before applying for a visa, but there was a minimum of formalities. From our elegant old hotel (Czechs see to it that western tourists visit only the best hotels and restaurants) we took a streetcar to the Villa Bertramka which, because of Prague's growth in size, is now within the city limits. It is located in some rolling hills at the south end of town and, a rustic park surrounding it, the Villa seems quite isolated from the city.

The Czech government has gone to much trouble and expense to develop Bertramka into a fitting Mozart museum, for the .people still worship his music and consider him an adopted son of Prague. We strolled first through the music room which the master used. It is so well-preserved that it looks as though he has simply left the piano for a few moments and will return at any moment to take up his work again. Adjoining this is the Mozart sitting room whose hand-painted, open-beamed ceiling is singularly attractive.

Other rooms in the home have the appearance of a museum with showcases and exhibits. The garden behind the Villa contains the little stone table and bench at which Mozart purportedly composed most of *Don Giovanni.* Standing among a lush growth of trees and shrubs and looking at this little stone table in the fading light of day, I could almost feel the presence of the master.

A FINAL TRIBUTE

Undoubtedly the most tragic reminder of Mozart is the St. Mark's Cemetery on the outskirts of Vienna. As I stood at the iron grillwork of its main gate and looked over the green slopes and countless tombstones, it seemed incredible that one of the greatest geniuses that the world has ever known, a giant of music, could have been buried in a pauper's grave, unmarked by tombstone or cross. His widow did not even visit the cemetery until twenty years after his death!

Today there is one little hallowed spot of ground consecrated to Mozart; a little Baroque cherub of marble stands beside a broken column. The inscription is simple:

W. A. MOZART
1756-1791

Apartment house in Bonn where Beethoven was born, as seen from its own central courtyard. The window of the attic room in which the composer was born is located in the gable farthest to the right of the picture.

III
BEETHOVEN, THE STORY OF A TITAN

Bonn, now the bustling capital of the German Federal Republic, was once a quiet university town on the threshold of the Middle-Rhine. From it one looked north to unending plains and south to the gate-like opening between the legendary "Seven Mountains" and the volcanic Rodderberg. Here was the beginning of the "romantic country" whose beauty and charm were praised by writers and composers in poems and songs.

Unlike the majority of towns in central and southern Europe, Bonn has no secular buildings of Medieval, Renaissance, or early Baroque style. What was left after the wars of the seventeenth and eighteenth centuries was hardly more than a heap of ruins, among which perhaps twenty houses were left intact. The town was then completely rebuilt in the then new Rococo style. After the bombing raids of World War II, great portions of Bonn were once again razed. Fortunately the Rococo spirit was retained wherever possible while modern buildings were erected. As we wandered through the narrow, winding streets of the central section, we had a feeling of days gone by, for in spite of these new edifices and some large crowds, the old, small-town atmosphere of the late eighteenth century is still a pervasive part of Bonn.

Just down the street from the Jesuit Church, at No. 20 Bonngassee, is the little apartment building in which Ludwig van Beethoven was born in December of 1770. (The structure miraculously escaped wartime damage.) Although he only lived in this particular house until he was four years of age, it has been preserved since 1889 as a Beethoven Museum. It is here that one recaptures the spirit of this mighty Titan.

After having pulled the bell at the richly ornamented doorway, we were admitted to the large hall which extends across the breadth of the house according to the old custom. It

31

has a high, old-fashioned timbered ceiling and a picturesque staircase. On the right of the hall is a picture of the Blessed Virgin Mary in front of which, after Rhenish custom, a light in a red bowl is kept burning. We mounted the stairs to the rooms the Beethoven family occupied on the second and top floors. One of these is a tiny attic room with open-beam ceiling, sloping walls, and a gabled window. It was in this room that Ludwig was born; a rope across the doorway indicates that no one is permitted to enter this hallowed room. The only ornament in it is a bust of the composer made in the early nineteenth century by the Berlin sculptor Wolff and completed after the latter's death by his pupil Karl Voss.

We then descended one flight of stairs to the main living quarters the Beethovens once occupied. Here, in well arranged displays, are mementos, manuscripts, and portraits which clearly outline the composer's life. The brightly painted living room, which faces the garden of the inner court, contains the items associated with young Ludwig's days in Bonn: his father's writing desk and chair, a copy of one of Beethoven's first portraits, the original manuscripts of *A Knight's Ballet* (1791), a song "To Laura" (c. 1791) and *Rondo for Wind Instruments* (1792).

In the adjoining room, probably once a sleeping room, is the organ console on which Beethoven regularly played at the Church of the Minorites (now St. Remigius). The console was moved here when the church was modernized and has three manuals, pedal work and thirty-three registers. Ludwig was twelve when he first learned on this instrument.

The last of the three rooms of the original Beethoven apartment is now called "The Vienna Room." The square piano here, although not an authentic "Beethoven piano," dates from 1793 and is an excellent example of the early Viennese-mechanism. Portraits of Beethoven's Viennese associates hang on the walls: Archduke Rudolph, Haydn, Mozart, Clementi, Diabelli, Domenico Artaria (his first publisher), Rudolph Kreutzer, and Count Andreas Rasumovsky.

At the front of the building is the more spacious apartment of the former owner and Beethoven landlord. As we climbed the staircase to the third floor of this apartment we came upon a room divided only by the staircase itself. Originally this had been several rooms, but the partitions have been removed to make one large, bright room.

Our eyes immediately went to the handsome grand piano next to the window. We learned that the instrument had been built especially for Beethoven by the court piano manufacturer in Vienna, one Konrad Graf. Because the composer already was having grave difficulties with his hearing, Graf used four strings per key instead of the traditional three. Later, on the advice of Johann Mälzel (inventor of the metronome and a great friend of Beethoven) a large, curved hood of thin wood — similar to the top of a prompter's box in the theater — was made to direct more sound to the pianist. (This hood is no longer in existence.)

Between the windows on the street side of this room is a glass showcase containing the quartet of string instruments that Prince Karl Lichnowsky gave Beethoven in the year 1800: an Amati violin of 1690, a Guarnerius violin of 1718, a Rugero viola of 1690, and a Guarnerius cello dated 1675. The first time I visited this museum I asked the Curator if these instruments were ever removed from the showcase and played so that the famous wood and varnish would stay alive. He replied, "Oh, yes! Why, only last week Casals stopped by and played the cello for a few hours."

Portraits of Beethoven adorn the walls of the room; some are the originals, others are excellent copies. The one by Ferdinand Schimon (in which Beethoven holds his manuscript of the *Missa Solemnis*) was said by his contemporaries to be the best likeness. Schimon was a musician (singer) as well as painter; he started the portrait in 1818, but Beethoven, busily at work on his *Missa Solemnis*, refused to sit for him. At the special request of the artist, the composer allowed him to erect his easel in the room adjoining his study. Schimon worked in this manner until the picture was nearly completed except for the eyes. The painter's easy-going, almost blunt manners — of arriving, for

33

The garret room in which Beethoven was born. A single bust with a laurel wreath at its base is the only thing now to be seen in the room.

The Beethoven Museum in Bonn has on display one of Beethoven's favorite pianos, built for him by Konrad Graf with four strings for each key in order to compensate for Beethoven's failing hearing.

example, without even wishing Beethoven "good morning" or of making himself at home as if it were his own studio — aroused the composer's curiosity to such an extent that he invited the young man to have coffee with him. Schimon made use of such invitations to "sixty coffee beans" to study Beethoven's eyes carefully, and so was able to finish the work "quite to Beethoven's satisfaction."

Unquestionably the most heartrending display in the room is the one devoted to the hearing aids Mälzel built for Beethoven over a period of several years. The first one dates from 1811 and is quite small, being in the traditional shape of the old-fashioned ear-trumpet. These aids grow larger in size until the final one of 1814 is so large that it had to double back across the head of the composer for support.

In the same case is the death-mask, taken three days after the master's death, and after the post-mortem (in which both the inner and outer ears were removed for scientific study).

Other items on display in this room include the surreptitiously made sketch of Beethoven on his death bed (not discovered until 1910), several locks of the master's hair, two pair of his spectacles, a monocle which Beethoven used for years, and his pen and inkwell. Several objects from Beethoven's desk are also on display: a clock in the shape of an inverted pyramid, a bronze lampstand, a small porcelain bust of Brutus, a table bell, two Russian paper weights given him by Prince Rasumowsky, two seals, and the copper plate used for engraving his calling cards. Beethoven's walking stick — the one seen in most of the portraits — is on display, also. It is made of simple bamboo with a small silver plate bearing the master's name at the upper end.

IN AND AROUND BONN

Within walking distance of the Beethoven museum are several buildings that reflect the spirit of the composer's era. The most impressive is the University of Bonn which is picturesquely situated on the bank of the Rhine. In the master's day this was the Residenz, the court at which his grandfather served as Kapelmeister and for which his father was hired as a tenor. Like the old city hall (now the post office) the Residenz is ochre in color (sometimes called "Maria Theresa yellow") with white trim and green roof. Beautifully landscaped, spacious in its layout, the Residenz suggests a more leisurely way of life and the importance in days gone by of even minor nobility. It was here that Beethoven first formally studied music with Neefe.

South of Bonn — perhaps five miles — is the town of Godesburg where most of the foreign embassies are now located. Driving in a westerly direction from this city toward the foothills, we came upon the ancient Cloister of Marienforst, a spot which used to attract Beethoven on his rambles. He once played a newly reconditioned organ in the Marienforst chapel to the interest and amazement of the peasants who lived there. The chapel has long since disappeared, but the barnyards and the surrounding little cottages still remain. It was fun to walk among these ancient buildings, looking at the chickens, the horses, and cows whose coops and stables still share the same roof as their peasant owners. Since this is a spot probably never visited by the citizens of Godesburg, let alone foreign tourists, the peasants looked out of their windows in bewilderment at us, probably as an earlier generation had looked at Beethoven in awe when he had the temerity to play the pipe organ in their chapel.

The Kreuzberg Monastery is not far away; it is a spot that used to attract Ludwig and his friend Stephen von Breuning on their long walks together. The monastery is in a better state of preservation than the Cloister, and is hidden in a lush growth of trees and shrubberies far back into the hills west of Godesburg. Of particular interest is the Santa Scala, the "Sacred Stairway" — a long, marble staircase which leads to the chapel. With arched windows on either side of the broad stairway of more than twenty-five steps, the frescoed ceiling abounds in cherubs and saints depicted in the Baroque style.

36

Organ console on which Beethoven learned to play the pipe
organ and on which he earned his first money as a professional
musician playing for church services. It was, in his day, located
in the choir loft of the Minoritenkirche in Bonn; today it is on
display in the Beethovenhaus, Bonn.

37

BEETHOVEN'S FOREBEARS

On our pilgrimage around Europe we had arranged to spend a few days of rest with some friends in Belgium, a professor and his wife. They live in Mechelen, about a half-hour's ride by express train from Brussels, and a spot almost never visited by American tourists. Although Mechelen today has more than 60,000 inhabitants, it is a very old town dating back to medieval times. The buildings in the central section attest to this age, for they have facades designed in the ancient Dutch-Flemish tradition. The narrow, cobblestone streets wind in and about; the professor carefully told us that this was an intentional part of their design. When the streets were first laid out, it was thought — in the best military fashion of the day — to make no straight section longer than the effective firing range of the primitive weapons then in use.

Although we had planned no musical activities or research efforts while in Mechelen — rather intending to enjoy a relaxed home atmosphere and some wonderful Flemish cooking — our curiosity was piqued one day as we passed a street named *Beethovenstraat*. Our friend gave us an answer: it was in an old home but a block down this street that Ludwig van Beethoven was born. I tried tactfully to correct the professor by saying that Ludwig was born in Bonn, Germany; his reply startled me. "That," he patiently explained, "was his grandson! The old man was born right here in Mechelen."

We wandered down the street to the site where the house once stood, now marked by a plaque. It seems that even in Mechelen the wheels of progress and industry churn on, for the old Beethoven house was razed in 1930 to make room for the expansion of the local brewery, one of the most famous in Europe (Lamot beer if your taste lies in this direction). Across the street is an ancient beer cellar and restaurant in the best bohemian tradition. At the professor's suggestion we entered the beer cellar to look at a painting of the grandson, the composer and namesake of the Mechelen Beethoven. I was quite shocked when I saw the painting, for although I am no art connoisseur, it appeared that this was an original portrait of ancient vintage, not a copy or reproduction. What surprised me was that this seemed to be the missing portrait for which I had finally given up a search. The original had been painted by G. Ferdinand Waldmüller (in 1823) on commission from the music publishers Breitkopf und Härtel. Apparently the copy in the Bonn Museum was made in the music publisher's offices late in the nineteenth century. From correspondence with Breitkopf und Härtel in East Germany, I had learned that the original was lost, stolen, or destroyed during World War II. Could this be the original that I had discovered in Mechelen? The owner of the beer cellar, who gave me permission to photograph both the cellar and the portrait, refused to answer any questions concerning the origin of this particular painting or state whether this was an original or a copy.

VIENNA, CITY OF UNFULFILLED DREAMS

Beethoven was twenty-two when he moved to Vienna; during the thirty-five years he lived in the Austrian capital he changed his lodgings on the average of twice a year. Any good guide book that one purchases in Vienna will list from a half-dozen to twenty or more existing buildings in which the master once lived. One can develop bunions and callouses trying to track down all of these; and most of them are not that important or significant. A few of the ones we visited merit special mention.

Probably the most interesting are those located in the Heiligenstadt area. This section of Vienna still seems remote, as though one were in a small country village. The streets wander among one and two-storied stuccoed buildings with shingled roofs. Many of these small homes are painted in pastel blues or pinks or yellows. Trees line the sides of the streets which are illuminated by quaint gaslights at night. Rustic tranquillity and serenity permeate the atmosphere.

Beethoven fled Vienna during the autumn of 1802 to

Heiligenstadt to occupy the house which is today No. 6, Probugasse. In the courtyard of this little two-storied house the master attempted to complete his second symphony and to get the rest his doctor had prescribed for his hearing malady. In desperation Beethoven took pen in hand a few weeks later to write those words which have since come to be known as The Heiligenstadt Testament: "Even that courage which so often filled my heart during the long, glorious summer days,. has now fled. Oh Providence, grant me but one day of unclouded happiness, for true happiness has long since ceased to echo in my heart."

We walked a short distance to the house he occupied on the Pfarrplatz, now a little tavern. This was another reminder of Beethoven's earthly burdens, for it was while living here that he became ·the legal guardian of his nephew Karl, that scamp who plagued the master's life with his laziness, moral instability, and attempted suicide.

In central Vienna there are only two Beethoven residences of note. The first is the *Oberdöbling Haus* in which the *Eroica Symphony* was created. It is probably the drabbest, dirtiest looking building we saw in our travels, the most uninspiring and the most glum. It is only worthy of a visit (one cannot go inside as it is privately owned) to realize the extreme contrast between the physical structure itself and the mighty work of.art which took shape within its walls.

The *Pasquelati House* is also in central Vienna; this was a more pleasant visit for us. Built in 1791, the home originally belonged to Baron Pasquelati who had the large six-storied structure built high on the Molkerbastei, the medieval bastion that once surrounded the city of Vienna. Today this knoll overlooks Vienna's Ringstrasse, the broad, gently-curving boulevard that has replaced the old town walls. The worn stone steps of the spiral staircase lead up to Beethoven's apartment on the uppermost floor; because of the greater number of stairs to climb rent was always cheapest on the top floor. The two-room Beethoven apartment today is open to the public as a museum. There is little in the collection of special significance, but we

40

Beethoven-Grillparzer house in Vienna, where in 1808 both Ludwig van Beethoven and the poet Franz Grillparzer lived. The home is not too far from the Heiligenstadt district where Beethoven wrote his famous Testament.

Home of Beethoven's brother Johann in Gneixendorf, about fifty miles from Vienna, where the composer went for rest and relaxation during the last of his final, fatal illness.

41

were interested in the view from the windows, for Beethoven could look out at the nearby Danube and see the more distant Vienna woods stretching off in the distance.

Several of the palaces in which the master's music was first performed in his lifetime are now foreign embassies. Although they are not open to the public, it was interesting for us to see their attractive and detailed facades which form such a contrast to the plain and austere residences in which the composer lived. Among the more unusual were two in gaudy, Baroque style: the Palais Schwarzenburg (dating from 1697) and the Lobkowitz Palace (1687). The former Embassy of Imperial Russia, once occupied by Count Rasumovsky, was built in 1806 in neo-Greek style, and is currently being restored.

TOWARD THE END

We traveled in our rented automobile to the little village of Gneixendorf, about fifty miles northwest of Vienna, to see the home of Beethoven's brother Johann. The frame building with Mansard roof had originally been a manor house situated in the center of a rather large plot of land. As an apothecary, apparently Johann had sufficient income to afford one of the finest homes in the village. During Ludwig's final illness Johann invited the composer to come to Gneixendorf for a rest, saying that his wife could "take good care of her ailing brother-in-law."

Today this home is in a bad state of repair, occupied by a family that obviously cares little about the exterior appearance of the home. It had been raining the day we were there, and muddy, rutted roads led up to it; the land around the house itself was a quagmire. The dismal appearance of this house on such a cold and wet day suggested to us the chilly and indifferent reception that greeted Beethoven when he finally arrived here.

The Schwarzspanierhaus in Vienna, the master's last residence and the building in which he died, no longer exists, so we had only two places left to visit, the church where the funeral service took place and the graveyard where he was buried.

The Trinity Church of the Minorites was one of the most unusual church edifices we had ever seen. Its shape, which rambles off in all directions, beggars description. Some sections are round as in Medieval structures, other portions are square or hexagonal; the color of the original stone of which it was built could not be determined because of the years of filth and grime that have collected on their surface.

Originally Beethoven was buried in Währing Cemetery, but years later when it fell into neglect, the master's remains were transferred to the larger, more formal Central Cemetery. Today the Währing Cemetery grounds are a pleasant little neighborhood park, scarcely larger than a city block. The graves which we sought have been preserved off to one side of it. The original Beethoven tombstone rests but one grave removed from that of Schubert who asked to be buried near his idol. At the Beethoven graveside service, the composer's friend Grillparzer gave the eulogy, saying:

> "He was an artist; but he was also a man, a man in the fullest sense of the word. . . If he shunned the world, it was because in the depths of his loving nature he found no weapon to oppose her. If he avoided his fellow-men, he did so after he had given them his all and had received nothing in return. He remained alone, for he could not find another like himself. But to his dying day he preserved a loving heart toward all mankind, a fatherly affection for his own kin, and a kindliness for the whole world. − Thus he lived and died, and thus he will remain for all time."

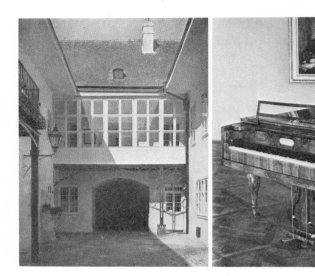

Courtyard of the apartment house in which Schubert was born, looking toward the street.

Schubert's grand piano made in Vienna by Johann Alois Graf.

Birthplace of Franz Schubert, a 16-unit, two-storey apartment house built in the shape of a U around a central courtyard (seen above left.) Each unit consisted of a living room and kitchen.

IV
SCHUBERT: A TRUE BOHEMIAN

The earliest use in English[1] of the word bohemian to describe a mode of living occurs in Thackeray's *Vanity Fair* of 1848: "She was of a wild roving nature, inherited from mother and father, who were both Bohemians, by taste and circumstances." Fourteen years later the Westminster Review acknowledged the general use of the word when it said that "the term 'Bohemian' has come to be very commonly accepted in our day as the description of a certain kind of literary gipsey, no matter in what language he speaks, or what city he inhabits. A Bohemian is simply and artist . . . who, consciously or unconsciously, secedes from conventionality."

[1] In French the word *bohemienne* has been used since the 15th century to identify gypsies because it was believed that these nomads either came from Bohemia or had passed through there enroute to Europe. Henri Murger's novel, *La Vie de boheme* (on which Puccini's opera is based), was published in 1851.

The more I read about the life of Franz Schubert – and I have researched every biography in English – the more it seems to me that this gentle soul, born in 1797, must have been one of the precursors of this non-conformist movement. As we started on our pilgrimage by following Schubert's path in and around Vienna, I became even more convinced. Consider these facts: he was gainfully employed for less than three years of his life; he lived in seventeen lodgings within a ten-year period; he composed on impulse, when inspired. Only one of his major works and none of the shorter pieces was composed on commission, by request, or for a specific purpose.

His was not a disciplined nature. He seldom made corrections in works once they were written down, and he encountered the most difficulty with the larger, more involved forms (*i.e.*, the piano sonatas). He defied convention by writing a symphony in two movements which program annotators persist in calling the "unfinished" symphony. (What could be more perfect than

45

these two beautifully balanced movements?) He composed a string quartet in one movement, since called *Quartettesatz*, meaning a movement of a quartet. (What a complete gem this work is!)

Truly, Schubert lived a life of musical beauty and physical ugliness. Our travels led us from one dreary, drab building to another. Not even the church where his funeral was held — and Vienna abounds in resplendent churches — was in the least attractive.

THE "RED CRAYFISH"

The house in which Franz Schubert was born was, in his day, on the outer fringes of Vienna, a little suburb of 7000 inhabitants called Liechtental. Today, because of the growth of Vienna, the building is a part of the city's ninth district, easily reached by automobile or streetcar.

Then known as *The Red Crayfish*, this dwelling was built sometime before 1780. It had three basement rooms of which one belonged to the landlord, a master mason. The ground floor, at that time without shutters, and the second story contained no fewer than sixteen apartments, each consisting of a living room and a kitchen. The elder Franz Schubert (the composer's father) moved his family into this building in 1786, just a year before his famous son was born.

The Red Crayfish — a dirty grey-brown in color in spite of its name — is built flush with the roadway and has two wings with a courtyard between. Originally the upper floor was reached by a stone stairway at the front; during the late nineteenth century an open stairway was constructed in the courtyard. It is now acknowledged that the elder Schubert taught school in the last lodging but one in the courtyard to the right. He taught more than forty pupils in the room-and-a-half combination and had to pay out of his own pocket to have them remodeled to accommodate his school. The family lived on the upper floor, on the street side of the right wing. I could hardly believe that, in addition to Ignaz who was born before the family moved

46

here, Schubert's mother, in one room and a kitchen, bore a further twelve children and provided for the five who survived infancy.

Because The Red Crayfish was an inexpensively constructed building, it easily fell into disrepair in the nineteenth century. In May of 1905 the City of Vienna purchased the building so as to preserve Schubert's birthplace for posterity. It was opened as a museum in 1912. Under the guidance of the great Schubert scholar, Otto Erich Deutsch, the museum was renovated in 1952 in an attempt to make the building's appearance more like that of 1786; it was then redecorated in 1962. By 1965 the City of Vienna found it necessary to close the building altogether because of structural weaknesses.

Today the left side of the main floor is occupied by an optician, while a tobacconist's shop may be found on the right side. The central doorway is barred; a little sign on it informs the tourist that the upper floor has been condemned and that the second-floor Schubert apartment — which is now the museum — is closed until the city can reconstruct the building. None of the city officials to whom I spoke seemed to know when the money to accomplish this could be raised and work begun.

Fortunately when I first visited the museum in 1955, it was open to the public. The kitchen of the Schubert apartment served as a cloakroom, while the living room housed the museum. Except for some chairs, the only item of furniture in the room was Schubert's grand piano. Accustomed to the American museum's "do not touch" policy, I was pleasantly surprised when, after a conversation with the curator, it was suggested that I sit down and play this piano. What a thrill it was as I went through one of the *Impromptus* to realize that my fingers were touching the same keys that his had played, that my ears were hearing music from the same instrument that he had heard.

All the important and authentic portraits of Schubert were on display. There are not many of them since the composer did not achieve widespread fame in his lifetime. The most beautiful,

47

as well as most authentic portrait, is in a watercolor by Rieder; an engraving of it was made by Passini around 1825 and published three years before Schubert's untimely death. There are three pictures that suggest Schubert's long association with his fellow bohemians — artists, poets, minor composers, and singers. First is Kupelwieser's watercolor of 1820, *Excursion by the Schubertians*; next is the same artist's watercolor of 1821, *Charades by the Schubertians*; and lastly von Schwind's incomplete sepia drawing of 1868 (made long after the composer's death), *A Schubert Evening at Spaun's*.

A few blocks away, down a little hill, is the Liechtental Parish Church, built in 1712. The composer, along with all his brothers and sisters, was baptized here. Later, his father sent him to sing with its choir and to study the pipe organ and thoroughbass with the choirmaster. It is a typical parish church of late Baroque design with little to distinguish it from its counterpart in other suburbs of Vienna. Perhaps the one unusual thing about its highly decorated interior that catches the eye of an American is the use of crystal chandeliers. There is a certain charm about this small church, almost an intimate atmosphere, and it is not difficult to imagine the seventeen-year-old Franz walking a few blocks from his home to conduct the performance of his first Mass in this church.

OTHER SCHUBERT DWELLINGS

A short walk took us to No. 3 Säulengasse, *The Black Horse*, the home that the elder Schubert purchased in 1801. He installed his family in the second-floor rooms while his school, now numbering some 300 students, occupied the main floor. The building is considerably bigger than The Red Crayfish, with larger apartments inside, but actually more dingy in appearance. Apparently the building is no longer in use, its rooms unoccupied. Traces of letters which were once appliqued to the front (and which have now been removed) indicate that the structure was recently used as a commercial building. Many

Main entrance to Vienna's Kaiserlich-Königliches Stadtkonvikt, or "The Imperial and Royal City Seminary" where Schubert lived for five years as a singer in the Imperial Choir (now the "Vienna Boys' Choir").

Steyr, Upper Austria, picturesquely situated on the Enns River. During one of his holidays here Schubert wrote his *"Trout Quintet"* at the request of one of the town's amateur cellists.

shingles of the roof are now missing and the dun-colored plaster is falling off its exterior walls.

From this home Schubert was sent to the Konvict, or Royal Choir Training School. The Konvict is in central Vienna, adjacent to the Old University. There are four floors to this building, whose exterior is also in a sad state of repair — plaster peeling away, dirt spattered around its base from the water of many a winter's storm. The facade is absolutely plain, just a series of windows in a solid wall. It reminded us of some of the contemporary crackerbox hotels. Schubert frequently complained of being cold and miserable while living and studying here; certainly nothing was done by way of decor or color to make this plain building any more attractive, warm, or cheerful.

Next in the Schubert chronology comes the St. Anne's Training School where his father sent him to finish his preparation for teaching once he had been released from the Royal Choir School. It is only a short distance from the Säulengasse home and of the same plain, simple architecture. Built out to the street's edge as are all the buildings in the district, it is undistinguished and somber in appearance.

From St. Anne's the composer returned to the Säulengasse home where he served as his father's teaching assistant for less than three years. At that point Schubert gave up and was never gainfully employed again. During this time (1813–1816) the composer, in addition to teaching reading to the first and second grades, composed no fewer than 400 of his grand total of about a thousand works: four symphonies, three Masses, three operas, two string quartets, and more than 250 songs including *The Erlking*.

For the next ten years — the last years of his life — he lodged first with one friend and then another, a total of seventeen different residences. Professor Watteroth's home in whose courtyard Schubert's first cantata (*Prometheus*) was performed, is still extant although it will soon be razed to make way for a more modern and larger building. Schubert then moved to the *Fruhwirthaus*, next to the beautiful St. Charles' Church, so that he would be only a few doors away from the residence of his

Bad Gastein, a health spa located high in the Alps south of
Salzburg. Vogl and Schubert visited this idyllic retreat shortly
before the composer's early death at 31. The two occupied rooms
that overlook the falls in the hotel to the left of the bridge. While
Vogl took "the cure" for his gout, Schubert composed several
small works in his hotel room and worked on a symphony (of which
no trace has ever been found.)

friend Moritz von Schwind. Today both buildings are gone, the Fruhwirthaus having been torn down in 1964. Nothing remained for us to see except a vacant lot.

Probably the most dismal of all the residences was *The Blue Hedgehog*, the former home of Franz Schober with whom Schubert lived in 1827 and 1828. Not only is the building falling apart and grimy in appearance, the present occupant has had the audacity to call it *The Schubert Garage*, and carcasses of old automobiles are to be found both in front of it and in the courtyard behind it.

The apartment of Schubert's brother Ferdinand, with whom he lived during the last year of his life, is preserved as a museum. By that we discovered it was meant that the two rooms were open to the public and for a few pennies admission one could go inside and see the room in which the composer died. Except for a few old copies of etchings of the composer and printed editions of his music nothing else is to be seen here.

By this time we were completely depressed. Unable mentally to reconstruct the milieu in which the composer moved because each residence was so discouraging in appearance, we thought we would visit some of the cafés that Schubert frequented. Two or three of them are still open, although their names have changed. No longer are they the gathering places for young artists and intellectuals, no longer are they alive with animated conversations. The neighborhoods in which they are located have declined and the taverns are now just stopping places for some of the oldtimers who want to drop in for a coffee or a beer. Even the atmosphere inside these cafés is of the plainest and simplest sort, nothing suggesting the *gemütlichkeit* of the early nineteenth-century Vienna.

Our visit to Schubert residences would not have been complete without a stop at Vienna's General Hospital where the composer spent the unhappiest days of his life in an effort to effect a cure for the syphylis that he had contacted. (Once again the idea of the bohemian came to mind, for to this day no one knows from what contact Schubert was infected with this dread social disease.) The hospital occupies all of one city block, a two-story structure of the traditional brownish-grey stuccoed exterior. We were told that the Viennese soon hope to build a new general hospital since this one has been in use for more than two hundred years and is outdated as well as overcrowded. Here, within these walls, Schubert completed his song cycle *Die Winterreise* while a patient.

EXCURSIONS OUTSIDE VIENNA

Probably Schubert's happiest days were those spent on short excursions away from Vienna. He made several delightful trips to the ancient town of Steyr, about seventy-five miles west of Vienna. It is a picturesque medieval town on the Enns River and is built around a central market square. Just opposite the sparkling fountain in the square is the old house of stone, No. 32, in which Schubert always stayed. The shops on the ground floor of that building (the composer occupied a third-floor residence) along with the adjoining stores are like chapters out of the past, for this sleepy, leisurely community seems to have been bypassed by the twentieth century.

Another interesting excursion was to Ochsenburg Castle, near St. Pölten to whose bishop the Castle belonged in Schubert's time. One of the Schubertians was a nephew of the bishop and arranged for all the group to spend a holiday there. The castle, about forty miles west of Vienna, is situated on the crest of a dome-shaped mountain; it is so completely surrounded by a deep forest of trees that we could see only its red-tiled roof from the distance. As we drove closer, the castle was totally obscured by the trees until we were within a hundred feet of it.

An old moat, now dry, still surrounds the sturdy walls of the castle, and we noticed that its present owner uses it as a dog run for his pets. While the Schubertians were visiting, Franz would spend the morning in his room composing. Then the whole group would gather for an outing in the afternoon — frequently by carriage. The evenings were devoted to performances of the composer's music and then perhaps a game of charades.

53

The most pleasant part of our Schubert pilgrimage was the retracing of the trip the composer made with his friend Vogl to Salzburg and Bad Gastein, the longest trip of his life. Schubert was so enthralled by the holiday that he wrote a rather vivid description of it in a letter to his brother.

"Our journey brings us first to Kremsmünster," Schubert wrote. "Here there is a lovely valley with a few small, gentle rolling hills. On the summit of one is a large monastery that offers the most spectacular view." That monastery today is still perched high above the Krems River, with the village itself crowded around its base on the banks of the river. Like the great Baroque church of the monastery, the homes and shops have red tile roofs and beige or grey stuccoed walls.

A short distance away is the town of Gmunden, situated on the most northerly shore of the Traun Sea. This large lake then wanders among the rugged mountains that surround it down to the city of Bad Ischl on its south shore, some ten miles away. "The countryside is truly magnificent and moves me deeply," the composer confided to his brother. "I have been here six weeks. If you could only see these wonderful mountains and lakes that threaten to engulf us. Vogl and I are staying with some of his friends, and each night we make music. My songs from 'The Lady of the Lake' by Sir Walter Scott are particularly popular."

We parked our car on the tree-shaded lane that parallels the lake's shore and then walked down to the water's edge. Schubert had not exaggerated the beauty of this area. He had failed to mention, though, the quaint little Baroque church that stands on an island just about a hundred yards off shore. Man's tribute to God seemed so small and insignificant compared to the lofty peaks and vast expanse of water the Creator had provided for man.

Regretfully we left Gmunden and headed west toward Salzburg, finally entering the Tyrolean countryside. No better description of our twentieth-century reaction to this region could be given than the composer's account of more than 150 years earlier:

"On our way through the country we saw houses of unique architecture. Nearly everything was made of wood. Wooden kitchen utensils stood on wooden trestles fixed on the outside of the houses, around which ran wooden balconies. The homes often had dates from the 1500's and 1600's carved over their doorways!

"The wide, isolated valley, dotted with castles, churches and farms opened up before our enchanted eyes. Towers and palaces gradually appeared. Eventually we entered the town of Salzburg through splendid avenues. [Here we must interpose a twentieth-century veiw. The streets seemed very narrow by contemporary standards.] Houses of four or five storeys filled the wide streets. We crossed the churning, dark waters of the Salzach river.

"Here in Salzburg Vogl sang some of my songs. My *Ave Maria* moved the audiences very much."

After we had stayed in Salzburg for several days we decided to make the journey to Bad Gastein where Schubert and Vogl had gone so that Vogl could "take the cure" in the mineral waters of that resort. Gastein is only forty miles south of Salzburg, but because the road is constantly climbing higher and deeper into the Alps, and because narrow curve follows narrow curve, it took us almost three hours to make the trip by automobile.

The city is situated on the very steep side of a mountain; the waterfalls — a series of one after another, tumbling down more than four or five hundred feet in its path through Gastein — bisects the town. The handsome Hotel Straubinger is located in the upper section of the city, and the water plummets in mighty cascades just under its windows. A plaque near the carriage entrance to the hotel commemorates the quartet that Schubert composed there.

We were unable to determine if that hotel had been reconstructed or enlarged since Schubert and Vogl were residents. Certainly it is one of the best and most elegant hotels in the town. Either Vogl had the money to pay for a very exclusive hotel, or else it has been rebuilt in the last hundred years in a more ostentatious fashion. No word is to be found on the plaque, and none of the local citizens seems to know, of the symphony that Schubert is purported to have composed in his hotel room while Vogl was taking the waters, a work to which the composer referred in a letter as his "Gastein symphony, my best work in this form." Like the music — if ever there was such a work — the memory of it has disappeared from this resort community.

THE WAHRING CEMETERY

Grave hunting is at best a gruesome pastime to my way of thinking. On our musical pilgrimage we encountered all types of morbid experiences. Haydn's head was separated from his body at death and they were not reunited for burial for another two hundred years. Mozart's grave, of course, was never marked and remains to this day unknown. Verdi and his wife were placed in crypts in the home he built for aged musicians, while Puccini, his wife, and son are crammed into the wall of his home directly behind his old Forester piano. Wagner's grave is covered by a plain stone, with neither date nor name on it, although just four feet away his dog is buried with a traditional gravestone on which is carved the animal's name and dates.

However, with Schubert I found an exception to this odious type of quest.

The little Währing Cemetery — or at least what is left of it — hints strongly of the spirit of this master of melody. I felt that after having pursued Schubert's path in and out of more than a score of residences, churches, and schools, I had finally come upon a hallowed spot, a consecrated memorial that was the quintessence of his mortal life.

56

The General Hospital in Vienna dates from 1783 and is still in use as the University Clinic for the training of doctors. Schubert was confined here in 1823 with a serious attack of syphilis.

The original grave of Beethoven (stone marker on left) separated by one from the grave of Schubert (Greek columns and pediment over a bust cast in iron by Josef Alois Dialer in 1829.)

57

Long ago, his remains, along with those of Beethoven, were transferred to the enormous Central Cemetery. The neighborhood around the Währing Cemetery had become less than the best residential district, and the cemetery itself had fallen into neglect. Fortunately when the transfer was made in 1888, the original gravestones and tombstones of one little section were preserved.

Today the former cemetery is called *The Schubert Park*. It occupies an entire city block and its tree-shaded paths provide a haven for the tired, the indigent. They stoll down its lanes or rest on its benches. That which provided the only material beauty in Schubert's life − nature itself − provides the setting: green patches of lawn, colorful beds of brightly blooming flowers, tall, stately trees. Birds sing overhead in the branches of maples and poplars, shutting out the sounds of the busy city and noisy streets that surround the park.

On the east edge of it is a path leading past the only remaining gravestones. The largest one, with a stately column rising above it, is Beethoven's. Schubert worshipped this man. "After Beethoven, who can compose?" he asked. Later the younger composer served as a torchbearer for the titan's funeral, an insignificant post in a lavish and highly organized procession. It was not beneath Schubert's dignity; he would do anything to pay his loyal respects to the master.

When Schubert's final hour was approaching − as it did all too soon − he asked his brother to inter him after his death next to Beethoven. Unfortunately in that brief period somebody had been buried in the plot next to Beethoven. So Schubert was buried one grave removed. And so it remains today.

A low wrought-iron fence surrounds the grave. The tombstone is classic, yet simple. Framed by Ionic columns capped by a pointed pediment is the bust of Schubert carved by the Tyrolean, Josef Alois Dialer, who had known the composer and perhaps had taken a death mask of him. It is a youthful and handsome Schubert that is depicted, rugged yet sympathetic. It is the most inspiring likeness of the composer.

Needless to say, I did not go to the Central Cemetery to see the more ornate and pretentious cenotaph. Here at the Währing Cemetery I had found the simple burial site, the one the master had requested.

Birthplace of Giuseppe Verdi, Le Roncole. The composer was born in a small room on the second floor whose only window is the one to the extreme right. His father's tavern/grocery store occupied the ground floor wing to the left.

Room in which Giuseppe Verdi was born on October 10, 1814. All the original furniture has long since disappeared. Today, on a table, rests a register signed by visitors; among the signatures are those of a dictator, a king, a pope, and composers and opera stars.

V
VERDI: GENTLEMAN FARMER, COMPOSER

"I had a hard time of it as a boy," Giuseppe Verdi told one of his friends in later life. "I was born poor in a most impoverished little village."

That little village, Le Roncole, is today hardly more prosperous than it must have been then. It lies on the eastern edge of the former Duchy of Parma, and it was from Parma that we started on our pilgrimage.

We drove the twenty-two miles over a little, two-lane country road; we were in the heart of the Po valley. Here in winter, bleak mists sweep over the flat plains, but on this sunny summer's day the rich farmlands were abundant with green fields of sugar beets. One farmer's acreage in this countryside is separated from the next by straight rows of tall, leafy trees. When we finally reached Le Roncole, we discovered it to be — even today — the smallest of hamlets. There are a few dozen buildings, and, where two roads meet, a tavern. It was in this solid but crude structure that Giuseppe Verdi was born on the 13th of October, 1813.

The grounds around the building are well maintained, and bright red and yellow cannas were blooming in the front yard. The garden is kept fresh and green by water drawn from the same well once used by the Verdis.

Much of the ancient stucco has fallen away from the outside walls of the building itself, revealing the earthen brick of which it is built. A vaulted store to the left served as Carlo Verdi's tavern and village grocery. Now that this humble abode is a national monument, the father's *osteria* lodges the custodian and his family. We entered a small hallway and climbed the rustic stairs to the upper floor which was formerly the Verdis' living quarters.

61

We looked first at the room in which the composer was born; it was very small, with rough plastered walls and an open-beamed ceiling of hand-hewn oak. One could imagine how bleak and dreary this dark bedroom must have been in winter with so little light coming from its one small window. It was undoubtedly cold, too, for the heating was inadequate and sweat formed on its old walls. In the adjoining room — once the Verdi parlor — we found this shrine's guest book. In it we discovered the signatures of a king, a cardinal, and a dictator in addition to those of numerous composers, singers, and conductors who have paid homage at this little tavern. Here in this room an attendant sells picture postcards of the building and photographs of Verdi in later life; she also collects a few pennies admission fee for the monument.

THE VILLAGE CHURCH

As we wandered out we saw directly across the roadway the village church, S. Michele, which played such an important part in the first years of Verdi's life. When he was less than a year old the advance units of the Russian and Austrian armies swept down across northern Italy, sacking and pillaging homes, raping and killing women. Le Roncole was directly in the army's path. When the church bell tolled the alarm, Luigia Verdi dashed across this roadway with her child in her arms. She climbed to the top of the church tower to hide, for she realized that the soldiers would search the sanctuary itself for victims. This act of wisdom and bravery probably saved the composer's life.

Later, in the loft of this very same church, Verdi learned the organ; at ten he earned his first salary playing for its services. As we paused to photograph this historic church, we saw a priest emerging from the doorway. He was followed by a group of young boys dressed in short pants and white shirts with black satin bow ties. Suddenly we realized that it was Sunday. One of the services must just have concluded.

Although both my partner and I are of Italian descent,

neither of us speaks the language. With trepidation I approached the Father to inquire if he would mind asking the boys to step aside so that we might take a picture of S. Michele. Nothing could have pleased him more than to learn that we wanted to photograph his church; he immediately beckoned the boys to move out of the way. While my partner took the photographs, the priest proceeded to tell me — with simple Italian words and much gesturing — the importance of this church in Verdi's life. He then urged us to go inside. First we had to sign the guest book in his little office. When he saw my signature, his eyes lit up. He proudly handed me his calling card: *Dom Adolfo Rossi.* We shared the same surname, and warm Italian abrazzos followed this discovery.

He now led us up a narrow wooden ladder somewhat flimsily attached to the wall. At the top there was a small hole, about four foot square, broken into the brick wall. As we crawled through it we discovered that we were in the organ loft. The priest insisted that I sit down and play, explaining that this was the very console at which young Verdi worked. He told us that the pipes had been restored and that the only change was the substitution of an electric blower for the old, manually operated bellows. Dom Adolfo pulled the stops — crude handles to the right of the keyboard — as I began to play. Overwhelmed by the emotional significance of this whole experience, I couldn't recall a note of music. I started to improvise from the manuscript on the music rack in front of me; it apparently was a setting of the Mass that had been used that morning. Unexpectedly the most beautiful sounds came from the chancel below. The boys we had seen earlier had re-entered the church. The Father, now leaning over the rail of the loft, was conducting them. I have never heard more heavenly voices, and the boy who sang the solo soprano passages was superb.

After we descended, Dom Adolfo explained how he had asked to be assigned to this church. He wanted to restore the old pipe organ and to make S. Michele a fitting tribute to the Maestro. The priest also told us how he had been instrumental

63

S. Michele, parish church of Le Roncole. Verdi was baptized in this church; within a year his mother hid with him in the tower of it to escape the hodes of the Russian and Austrian armies that were approaching the village.

The organ loft and altar, S. Michele. Verdi took his first pipe organ lessons on this instrument, and at ten years of age received his first professional appointment as organist for this church.

in getting the Italian senate to change the name of the village. Thanks to the enthusiasm and efforts of our newfound friend, the hamlet is now known officially as *Le Roncole-Verdi*.

VERDI LEAVES HOME

Giuseppe did not give up his organist post when, at ten, his father sent him to the nearby village of Busseto to study. Twice a week he walked the three miles each way so that he could play for the church services in Le Roncole. The story is well known how Verdi, in returning one dark and stormy night, fell into one of the drainage ditches at the side of the road and perhaps would have perished had not a stranger come to his aid and pulled him out.

As we drove the short distance to Busseto this story was constantly on my mind, for deep culverts still parallel the elevated roadway on both sides, separating it from the flat farmlands that stretch off to the horizon.

We parked our car on the outskirts of Busseto. The town is not large — perhaps a few thousand inhabitants — but it must have seemed enormous to the lad from Le Roncole. Although there are a number of streets in Busseto, most of the stores line its principal one which leads to the piazza. The shops were closed as it was Sunday, but vendor's stands lined both sides, the proprietors hawking their wares: shoes, kerchiefs, soft drinks.

This main thoroughfare was filled with the men of the village; women, in the Italian tradition, were nowhere to be seen. The men stood around in groups, some in the street, some on the sidewalks, talking, passing the time of day. Most were dressed in their Sunday suits which were neither stylish nor well-fitting since Busseto is not a prosperous town.

First we located the former home of Antonio Barezzi with whom Giuseppe lived, the man who, years later, Verdi came to call his "father, friend, and benefactor." Barezzi's status in Busseto is represented by the location of his house on the main

65

piazza (now named after the lad he took in). A plaque on the wall identifies it. Like all the stores on this street, it extends to the sidewalk's edge with an arcade built over it to give protection from the sun in summer and the rain in winter. These three-storied stuccoed buildings are painted in pastel shades: pink, blue, yellow, beige. Barrezi's is now a dusty rose color.

Barezzi ran a grocery store on the ground floor level of his home, a store that supplied Carlo Verdi's tavern. The living accommodations were on the second floor, and it was in one of the larger rooms that the local Philharmonic Society met once a week. Verdi had his first chance to conduct with this group, and his first instrumental music was written for these rehearsals in the Barezzi home. Although the functions of the building have changed over the years — the grocery store has now been transformed into the Busseto post office — the painted decorations inside the doorway are those that Verdi saw, including the illuminated initial *B* on the ceiling.

Further down on the same side of the street is the church of S. Bartholomeo. We supposed it to be a small, parish church. To our surprise we discovered, however, that the local citizens refer to it (somewhat euphemistically) as their cathedral! The design of this church is severe and angular. Neither energy nor money was wasted on supplying it with un-needed ornaments or embellishments. Its stuccoed walls blend into the pastel pattern of the village. Across the piazza is the Verdi Opera House. It was built late in the master's life, against his advice. He felt that Busseto needed to spend its hard-earned money for more essential civic improvements. Legend has it that he never set foot inside this opera house once it was completed, although years later his friend Arturo Toscanini gave several Verdi memorial performances in it.

Two former Verdi residences still exist in Busseto. The first is the Palazzo Tedaldi on a little side street near the town library. It is a square building of several floors; most of the paint is now peeling off its stuccoed walls. The shutters are in a bad state of repair. After Verdi returned from his studies in Milan, he

66

married his childhood sweetheart, Margherita Barezzi, and rented a small apartment in this building. They lived here for three happy years, moving to Milan at the end of that time only because it seemed more prudent if Verdi wished to see his operas produced.

Some fourteen years later, long after the tragic loss of his wife and two children, Verdi returned to Busseto and took up residence at the Palazzo Orlandi with the beautiful soprano Giuseppina Strepponi, his "Peppina" and future wife. The Palazzo Orlandi is just off the piazza. It is built of weathered brick and has an arcade of gently flowing arches.

THE VILLA SANT'AGATA

Since Busseto is a small town, gossip traveled about quickly and viciously concerning Verdi and his Peppina. In protest the composer stated that "neither she nor I owe any account of our actions to anyone. On the other hand, who knows what our relations are? Our business? Our connection? Or what claims I have on her and she on me? Who knows whether she is my wife or not? And who knows in this special case, what our thoughts and reasons for not making it public? . . . I demand my freedom of action because all people have a right to it."

To escape the charged atmosphere of Busseto, Verdi decided to buy some acreage and move out of town. Three miles to the north he discovered the estate of Sant'Agata and purchased it. The long and arduous task of fixing it up was described by Peppina in a letter to a friend:

"He bought the estate of Sant'Agata, and I — who had already furnished a house in Milan and another in Paris — had to arrange this spot for the illustrious professor from Le Ronchole. We began with great delight to plant a garden, which in theory, was called 'Peppina's garden.' It then grew in size and was called *his* garden; and I must say that in this garden of his he rules like a Czar while I am reduced to a few feet of

67

soil which he is forbidden to enter. I can't say that he always lives up to this agreement, but I have threatened to plant cabbages instead of roses.

"This garden, which kept on growing bigger and more handsome, then demanded a more dignified house, so Verdi became an architect. You cannot imagine the dances and promenades of bureaus, beds and tables that we went through. Suffice it to say that with the exception of the stables and cellar, we have eaten and slept in every nook in the house."

We had written ahead for permission to visit this villa; the Carrara Verdis (the composer's grand-niece and nephew) have inherited the home. During the winter they live in the second-floor rooms, keeping the Maestro's ground floor quarters — study, library, parlor, bedroom — just as he left them in the 1890's. In summer the Carrara Verdis move to Busseto so that the Villa can be opened to tourists. Signorina Carla Carrara Verdi, a very charming person with whom I conversed in French, accompanied us out to the Villa and asked the caretaker to show us about.

Weeping willow trees, planted by Verdi himself, stand beside the newel posts of the wrought-iron main gate. The gardens inside are beautifully kept, and, judging from old photographs taken in the 1880's, they must be similar to the ones the master maintained. The "mud puddle" which he turned into a scenic lake may still be seen as may the tall plane trees he planted beside the path leading to the fields. Just outside the front door to the Villa is a sand-covered court that was used for games of bocce ball, the Italian version of lawn bowling. An iron table and chairs to one side of the court look exactly like those that appear in an old photograph of Verdi and Boito taken one summer's afternoon in the garden when they were at work on *Falstaff*.

The house is of yellow stucco; long French windows with green shutters open from all the ground floor rooms into the garden. Giant magnolias as well as large shrubs shade the southern exposure of the home from the hot summer sun.

68

Gardens of the Villa Sant'agata. The gravel-covered courtyard in the foreground was used for games of bocce ball. The garden itself was designed and planted by the composer.

Parlor of the Villa Sant'agata. Portraits (including a steel engraving of William Shakespeare) and statuary are mounted on the wall above Verdi's favorite Erard piano.

Our first thought as we entered the house was how comfortably it was furnished. Although the style of the furniture is now out of favor, it was surely of the very finest when Peppina purchased it for Sant'Agata: overstuffed chairs and sofas, lace curtains with plush velvet drapes on either side, massive dark bedroom furniture. Everything is kept immaculately; nothing looks in the least like a museum.

In the large parlor Verdi's Erard piano may be seen; many pictures hang on the wall above it including a fine etching of William Shakespeare. A rather gruesome (at least to our way of thinking) plaster cast of the Maestro's right hand rests on his desk.

Verdi's hunting equipment is still kept in good order and his guns may be seen in the racks he used. There is a little study off his bedroom; his desk is placed right in front of the window. In this way he could survey the activities of his workmen and farmers while composing *Aïda* or *Otello*. To the right of the desk is a bookshelf containing his library of piano scores of operas by his contemporaries, including most of the works of Wagner.

The bedroom is dominated by the huge carved oak bed with massive canopy. Nearby, on a nightstand, is his set of the complete works of Shakespeare. The table at the foot of the bed is covered by portraits of his friends including one of Alessandro Manzoni. A huge marble bust of his Peppina commands the place of honor in this collection.

One room is devoted to his billiard table. A bookcase built into the wall of this room contains the popular novels of the day as well as the classical masterpieces of literature that the composer must have enjoyed reading.

The dining room is large — the table itself can seat a dozen or more guests — and the shelves of the sideboard are full of fine stemware and porcelain. "I ate too poorly in my youth to be able to give up the pleasure of eating fairly well now," Verdi commented to a friend.

For almost fifty years Verdi and his Peppina enjoyed this

home, although as they grew older they preferred to spend the cold and damp winter months in Genoa where the climate was milder.

VERDI AND MILAN

Reluctantly we left Sant'Agata and headed north on the Autostrada — the Italian expressway — for Milan. If the six-mile area from Le Roncole to Busseto and on to Sant'Agata had been the center of Verdi's personal life, Milan was the hub of Verdi's artistic career.

He traveled to Milan for the first time when he was eighteen to enroll at the Royal Conservatory of Music. When we located this conservatory that had turned Verdi away we felt it was most ironic that the sign over the door now reads *Conservatory Giuseppe Verdi!* The building is a large, square one of neo-Baroque design built around an arcaded central courtyard. The sounds that we heard as we looked about were similar to those heard at any school of music: passages being rehearsed on a half-dozen practise pianos, sounds of horns, strings, and winds coming from countless little studios.

We then drove downtown. The magnificent Gothic cathedral of Milan is the heart of the city. Across the street to the north is a huge, glass-domed arcade called *The Galleria*. Fine restaurants and expensive shops line the sides of its broad walkway. Completed just after Verdi moved to Milan, the composer used to enjoy an evening's promenade through it, as do the Milanese and tourists to this day.

At the far end of the Galleria is a piazza across whose broad square stands La Scala. The building itself is not impressive. The interior is traditional: the horseshoe curve of boxes above which the gallery is located, the whole dominated by the Royal Box in the center. Verdi's first opera, *Oberto*, was produced here, as were many of this more famous later works.

Many visitors and opera buffs are unaware of the wonderful Scala Theater Museum whose entrance is immediately to the

71

left of the Opera House itself. Its director, Giampiero Tintori, greeted us in his book-cluttered office. He explained to us that the idea of the Museum came about in 1911 when a number of men assocated with La Scala discovered that a huge auction of operatic memorabilia was to take place in Paris. Under the artistic direction of Arrigo Boito, these men were able to purchase the collection. The Museum was, after a series of postponements, officially opened to the public on the 8th of March, 1913.

Today the Museum houses a vast library of more than 80,000 books on opera, and includes displays devoted to musical archeology, ballet, costume design, and opera. Portraits of composers and singers adorn its walls, and a collection of famous musical instruments may be seen.

In the Verdi room we saw the Museum's most prized possession, the little spinet given the eight-year-old Giuseppe by his father. It was on this very instrument that the child made his first musical sounds, composed his first musical phrase. The term *spinet* may seem anachronistic for the 1820's but actually this instrument dates from the late 16th-century. It was originally a rough and rural spinet in contrast to the ornate and elegant ones that appeared in the palatial homes of the period. Probably Carlo Verdi, being unable to purchase an instrument to give his son, found one – perhaps given to him – that lay forgotten in some attic of a friend's home.

The spinet is small, the keyboard only four octaves. A childish hand has written on the white keys the names of the notes! On the lid rests the last key so that one can read the inscription on it: "I, Stefano Cavaletti, have repaired and recovered the hammers with new leathers, and have adjusted the pedal board [now missing]. I have done this work free of charge since I could see the desire that young Giuseppe Verdi has to play this instrument; this is payment enough for me and I am quite satisfied, Anno Domini 1821."

Near the spinet are showcases in which may be seen the items concerned with Verdi's days in Milan: the receipt for charges of his first wife's funeral; his passport (needed to travel

Master bedroom at Villa Sant'agata with its huge canopied bed with great velvet drapings. A bust of Giuseppina rests on the table at the foot of the bed along with copies of Verdi's favorite novels.

Cairo Opera House. The Khedive of Egypt built the opera house to coincide with the opening of the Suez canal. He then commissioned Verdi to compose an opera on an Egyptian subject for the formal dedication of the theatre. (*Adia* was the result.)

in those days from Busseto to Milan); a visiting card from Alessandro Manzoni; and Verdi's letter to Boito stating that he had just finished *Otello*. Nearby is the square piano that Barezzi gave young Verdi when he first came to Milan to study. The original full score of the *Manzoni Requiem* is also on display.

A wonderful collection of paintings hangs on the walls: portraits of Antonio Barezzi, Margherita Barezzi Verdi, two magnificent oils of Giuseppina Strepponi Verdi when she was a youthful and beautiful opera star, and of course, sketches of the Maestro himself.

LAND OF PYRAMIDS AND SPHINX

Although Verdi was commissioned to compose *Aida* to celebrate the completion of the Suez Canal and the opening of the new opera house the Khedive had built in Cairo, the Maestro did not make the long journey to see his opera produced. I had always been curious, though, to know what this opera house looked like. I had never been able to locate a description or photograph of it.

We made the lengthy plane flight to Egypt ostensibly to see this opera house, although we also wanted to visit the pyramids of Ghiza, the Sphynix, Memphis, and The Valley of the Kings. We found our trip down the Nile in a falukah (with the same native guide that had piloted the National Geographic party the year before) far more exciting than the Khedive's tribute to the world of opera. In typical European fashion, the opera house is located on the main square. It resembles a cross between the architecture of La Scala and Covent Garden. A rather drab grey in color, it was set off by splashing fountains in front surrounded by lush green flower beds. Since we were there the day after Independence Day, the house was decorated with a multitude of red, white, and black United Arab Republic flags. Relatively little use is made of the opera house these days; it was built in European style for a European art form that remains hostile to the Arabic culture. *Aida* was its one claim to fame.

74

LOYAL TRIBUTES

We turned from Egypt to Milan to visit the *Casa di Riposo*, Verdi's tribute to his beloved Giuseppina, his helpmate for more than fifty loyal, devoted, and loving years. The *Casa* is a home for aged musicians. Its design is typically late nineteenth-century neo-classical which to modern eyes looks not only passe, but ugly. A little arcade leads from the busy piazza on which it is located to a quiet, central courtyard which is filled with a cheerful garden, a spot of repose away from the clanging street cars and horn-honking automobiles that rush by in front of the building.

Just down the street from La Scala is the Grand Hotel Milano, the composer's last residence. After Giuseppina passed away, Verdi could no longer enjoy Sant'Agata. He rented a suite in this hotel. About a year and a half later (he was then 88) he suffered a massive stroke. Since all Milan knew that the Maestro lay fatally ill in his room, workers spread hay on the cobblestone streets in front of the hotel each morning so that the many carriages that passed up and down this busy thoroughfare would not disturb him with the noise made by their steel-rimmed wheels.

In an old Italian book I discovered Gabriel D'Annuzio's ode to Verdi. Its first stanza suggests the measure of the man:

He nurtured us as Nature's hand
Sustains mankind
With the free, encircling universe
Of air.

His life of beauty and manly strength
Alone
Swept high above us like the singing seas of heaven.
He found his song
In the very breath of the suffering throng.
Let mourning and hope echo forth:
He loved and wept for all men.

75

Entrance to Kreuz Grammar School in Dresden, Wagner's first school. He later said in his autobiography: "On the completion of my eighth year I was sent to the Kreuz Grammar School where, it was hoped, I would study!"

University of Leipzig. In 1830, Wagner informed his family that he had made up his mind not to study for a profession and would, instead, become a musician.

VI
WAGNER: POLITICIAN, POET, MUSICIAN, LOTHARIO

Like Napoleon, that other great egotistical tyrant before him, Richard Wagner seems to have left traces of his travels across the face of Europe in countless villages and cities. Such small towns as Moudon, Graupe, Laustadt, and Triebschen all boast memorabilia of his visits. The major cities in which the composer lodged and worked, of course, have their museums and Wagner exhibits: Leipzig, Dresden, Paris, London, Rome, Venice, Vienna, Munich, and Bayreuth.

Help from the composer's granddaughter, Friedelind Wagner, was obtained in planning this part of the musical pilgrimage. She had been in California, auditioning young singers for her master classes in opera at Bayreuth. She graciously gave of her time one afternoon to discuss her grandfather and his travels. Since he had been born in Leipzig and spent most of his youth either there or in Dresden, she suggested that East Germany would be a good place for us to start on our trek. I asked her about the formalities and difficulties in crossing behind the Iron Curtain; she assured me that the problems were minimal. She told me that she regularly takes her master classes each summer on an excursion to visit the Wagner shrines in East Germany and said that she had never encountered any problems.

Unfortunately, when we started on *our* Wagner pilgrimage, we hadn't yet learned one of the principal axioms for travelers to the communist areas: *Don't cross between east and west at the most controversial or troubled places on the frontier!* (Hungary and Haydn *should* have taught us this lesson!)

We flew to West Berlin from Brussels, for we had wanted to see for ourselves this outpost of democracy completely surrounded by communism. We then planned to cross into East Berlin and travel on to Dresden and Leipzig. Arrangements had been made through the Reisebüro, the government-operated travel agency for East Germany. Hotels had been booked and paid for; in addition, we also paid for all our meals plus the required "English-speaking guide with private transportation" for both cities.

When we left our West Berlin hotel on a Saturday morning the air was crisp and the sun was shining brightly. We hopped into one of the numerous taxis that seem to be ever present in West Berlin and asked the driver to take us to the Friederich-strasse crossing point, the one specified in our itinerary supplied by the East German travel agency. Our instructions said that we were to be met there precisely at ten o'clock by our guide. He would then take us to the proper offices to get our meal vouchers and hotel recéipts, then on to pick up our railway tickets and, finally, see that we got the necessary visas from the Polezei.

It turned out that the Friederichstrasse crossing point is *Checkpoint Charley.* Our driver was so fearful as we approached *the wall* that he slowed the taxi down to about 7 mph a considerable distance from it. He then wanted to let us out about four blocks away; since we had three large suitcases plus all our camera equipment with us, we kept encouraging him to continue on to the checkpoint. We were stopped by both British and French guards, for West Berlin is still "officially occupied" by the three Allied powers. After saluting in the best military tradition, both the French and English guards signaled us on after looking at our passports. Our last encounter with the Western authorities was with the American soldier on duty. When the taxi driver asked him in German where he should let us out, the GI replied, "Speak English, Mac, speak English. I don't understand this goddamn Kraut language."

As we entered the East German zone, we looked everywhere for our "English-speaking guide with private transportation." To this day we don't know what happened to him, but we never did find him. We realized, however, that if we were going to make the noon train for Dresden on which we had reservations, we had better find the Reisebüro and pick up our meal and travel vouchers without delay. I found a policeman and showed him the letterhead of our typed itinerary, asking him where the Reisebüro office was located. He told us that it was just down the street a few blocks. We hailed a cab, for the luggage was getting heavy, and found that "a few blocks" really amounted to "a few miles"!

The taxi stopped in front of a drab, tall structure. After paying the driver, we mounted the narrow stairs of this old building carrying all our bags with us as we didn't dare leave them on the street. I could tell as we walked into the third-floor office that we weren't in the proper one. A tired-looking secretary of rather ancient vintage sat at a lone typewriter. She informed us that her office was used simply as a clearing-house for mail, and that the Reiseburo office we wanted was just "a few blocks away."

Down the street, luggage in hand. The sun had disappeared and storm clouds filled the sky. Not a taxi to be seen. Eventually we reached the office to which we had been directed. We entered, and a pleasant young lady asked us to sit down in the waiting room for a few moments. She then disappeared with all our papers and passports into a back office. Minutes turned into an hour. Finally she emerged and handed us our vouchers for hotels and private guides. Our meal money was returned to us in East German *marks* at a most unfavorable rate of exchange. She then directed us to the Hotel Bertolina to pick up our railway tickets, urging us to hurry if we were going to make the noon train. We asked her to get us a taxi, for it had started to drizzle. The clerk apologized, saying that she doubted if she could get one for us as it was a "free Saturday," meaning a holiday for the *workers*. Because of the rain, she said that the few cabs still left on duty had probably stopped operating.

Fortunately she found one for us, and we dashed over to the Bertolina, leaving the taxi waiting for us while we picked up our railway tickets. The paper work that it took to get our reservations was unbelievable. Forms had to be filled out, various vouchers prepared, rates and schedules checked, the tickets written out. Finally they were handed to us. We bounded down the stairs to our waiting cab so that we could go to the Police Station for our visas.

By now the rain was really pouring down, so we tried to talk the taxi driver into waiting for us at the Police Station. He refused. We then unloaded the luggage and went into the office. There was a long line at the counter, filled with persons from Bulgaria, Roumania, and Czechoslovakia, all trying to get their visas renewed. We watched our train-time come and go as the line moved slowly forward. By 2:30 p.m. we reached the counter; we had done nothing for the past four and a half hours but stand in line or travel from one office to the next! When our turn came, our passports were checked against the master file of *persona non grata* in East Germany. Having passed this hurdle, the police clerk sat down at his desk to fill out the various required forms. My nerves — almost gone at this point — suggested a cigarette. Embarrassingly my lighter clicked and clicked, but still no flame. Slowly the police clerk pushed his chair away from the desk, sauntered over to the counter and lit my cigarette with his lighter!

Finally the visas were issued and we were back on the street, two forlorn-looking souls in the pouring rain in search of a taxi. It took us almost an hour to locate one. We headed for the depot, hoping that there would be a late afternoon train for Dresden. A friendly Information Agent at the station, who spoke excellent English, assured us that we could board a train about 5:30 p.m.

The three-hour train ride was rather pleasant and gave us a chance to see the countryside in this Saxon part of Germany. At Dresden we missed out "private transportation," which, in this case, *was* waiting for us. We went out the side door while our guide and driver waited for us at the main entrance! We checked in at the Gewandhaus, a completely remodeled hotel that had opened to tourists only six months earlier. Our English-speaking guide finally caught up with us there; because it was already evening, she arranged to meet us at ten o'clock the following morning. She said that she would give us two

The theatre at Lauchstädt in which Wagner conducted for the first time; it was a performance of Mozart's *Don Giovanni*.

The "Lohengrinhaus" in Graupa, near Dresden, in which the Wagners spent the summer of 1846 while the composer worked on *Lohengrin*. Today the small apartment on the top floor which Richard and Minna occupied is a Museum.

hours of her time — we had paid for a full day — and would provide a chauffeur-driven car for those two hours.

We then went to our rooms to clean up and relax before having a late supper. No amount of fiddling and fooling with the modern knobs on the shower would produce any hot water. I then tried the spigot in the wash basin and couldn't get anything but icy water out of that either. In desperation, I telephoned the desk to see if a porter could come up and show me the secret. The hotel manager apologized on the phone, saying that *the* hot water system for Dresden was closed down for two weeks while they did their annual pipe-cleaning operation. It was absolutely incredible! Here in this city of half a million people there was not a drop of hot water to be had for two weeks! Needless to say, the cold-water shower was extremely invigorating!

THE PILGRIMAGE BEGINS

We first visited the Zwinger Palace, a magnificent, sprawling rococo building on the southern bank of the Elbe River which flows through Dresden. Although more than three-quarters of the city was destroyed in World War II, this was one complex of buildings that escaped with only minor damage. The Zwinger was originally the seat of Saxon kings, and its countless rooms included audience chambers, ballrooms, music rooms, a theater and, of course, living quarters. It was for its theater that Wagner's stepfather, Ludwig Geyer, worked when Richard was a lad of five. Geyer "obtained a remunerative, respectable and permanent engagement as a character actor at the newly established Court Theater," Wagner later wrote. "My imagination at that time was deeply impressed by this theater, not only as a childish spectator from the mysterious stage-box, with its access to the stage, and by visits to the wardrobe with its fantastic costumes, wigs and other disguises, but also by taking part in the performance myself. . . . I remember that I appeared in. . . a piece especially written to welcome the King of Saxony on his return from captivity, with music by the conductor Carl

82

Maria von Weber. In this I figured in a lively tableau as an angel, sewn up in tights with wings on my back, in a graceful pose which I had laboriously practised."

The central courtyard of this palace — where Wagner as a child had heard his first band concert — was filled with Russian soldiers the first day that we were there, a Sunday. They had been trucked in to spend a brief leave viewing the art treasures of this fabulous museum. We must have been the only two Americans in Dresden, for as we wandered about the courtyard taking photographs of its splashing fountains and handsome statuary, we discovered that the Russian soldiers were busy taking pictures of *us*, probably to send back home to show their families what Americans *really* look like.

We next visited the Kreuzeschule which Wagner attended. "When I was eight," he later recalled, "I was sent to the Kreuzeschule in Dresden. . . . I was placed at the bottom of the lowest class. By the time I was in the fourth grade, I recited both 'Hector's Farewell' from the *Iliad* and Hamlet's celebrated 'Monologue' from memory. I was fascinated by history, mythology and legends. I also made some translations and wrote some original poems there, for it was clear to me that I was destined to be a poet."

The Kreuzeschule is not too far from the center of Dresden, located on a tree-shaded street now lined with fashionable private homes. The half-dozen blocks around the school is one of the few residential areas of the city that was not leveled by wartime bombing. The school building itself is large, stretching from one corner halfway down the block to the next. Built of grey stone, this three-storied edifice has a red-tile roof from which rises in the center a small, circular clock tower. A patch of green lawn extends from the wrought-iron fence at the sidewalk's edge up to the shrubs which surround the building itself. As schools go, this seemed to be an ideal spot: quiet, peaceful, a beautiful setting amidst treees and shrubs, and a cheerful building with many windows.

We returned to the center of town to visit the Kreuzekirke,

the parent institution of the school. Located on one of the main squares, the church, also of grey stone, is austere in appearance. The building is essentially square in shape; a tall belfry towers above its right side. Although the exterior of the church did not suffer too much from the bomb raids, the interior was gutted. The church is in constant use, but little has been done to restore the inside. The walls are of unfinished stone and brick, with little or no decoration except for the altar and a stained-glass window in honor of the church's former organist, Michael Praetorius.

We wanted to climb the stairs to the bell tower, but we were told that they were unsafe. It was from this belfry that Wagner, as a young man of thirty, watched for a day and an evening one of the first battles when the Prussians attempted to invade this Saxon capital. "I thought that by climbing the tower, I might get a good view of what was going on with the heavy firing of the Prussian advance artillery. At last the rifle fire was silent and the first attack exhausted itself."

It was shortly after this incident that Wagner and his young bride Minna moved. "In order to recover from my efforts of producing *Tännhauser* [in Dresden], I obtained a three-month leave. We moved to a little peasant's house in the village of Gros-Graupe. Here I hoped to improve my health in rustic retirement, and to get pure air to breath while composing my new opera."

We talked our guide and chauffeur into making the thirty-minute drive from Dresden to this little country village down the Elbe River. Graupe apparently has not changed much since the composer lodged there almost 120 years ago, for the few buildings in the hamlet are all old, and a quiet, rural atmosphere pervades the area.

A little pillar now marks the entrance to the farmhouse in which the Wagners lived; inscribed on it are the words, "Lohengrin — Parsifal," indicating in the following paragraph chisled out of stone that not only was the draft of *Lohengrin* completed here, but the idea for *Parsifal* also began to take form. We entered the carriage gate and approached the

The parlor of the "Lohengrinhaus" in Graupa, a room which doubled as a music room and study for the composer as he worked on his opera.

Villa Wahnfried, Bayreuth, the home Wagner designed himself; it was financed by his loyal patron, "Mad" King Ludwig II of Bavaria whose bust the composer placed on a pedestal in the courtyard.

house, a two-storey grey stucco building with red-slate roof. Entering its single door, we climbed the stairs to the two-room flat the Wagners had occupied. The parlor is a corner room, and the composer's square piano was located in the corner between the two small windows. A round oak table on which he worked is now covered with various editions of *Lohengrin*. To the table's side is a richly carved oak chair with mohair back and seat, one frequently used by Wagner when he lived there.

The former bedroom is now given over to a display of various portraits and photographs of the composer and productions of his operas. This miniature museum also has on exhibit handbills advertising the Dresden productions of his operas and copies of the many tracts that he wrote, some on politics, some on civil disorders, and one against the Jews and their power.

From Graupe the Wagners returned to the city. "The old Marcolini Palace in Dresden, with a very large garden laid out in the French' style, was located in an outlying and thinly populated suberb of Dresden. It had been sold to the town council and part of it was to be rented out. We moved into a spacious apartment of a side-wing of this palace. The large rooms served both for our living quarters and my studio."

Today the old palace is a hospital, and the city of Dresden has grown so much that this area is no longer a suburb. The building was designed in the Italian style then in favor, the wings being of stucco painted a "Maria Theresa yellow," while the entrance area behind a garden courtyard is built of sculptured grey sandstone richly carved.

LEIPZIG AND LAUSTADT

From Dresden we caught the train for the three-hour ride to Leipzig. The train had no sooner pulled into Leipzig — the largest station in Europe — than we saw an elderly little man pushing through the crowd, waving a small American flag (about the size of a calling card) high in the air. This was our guide for Leipzig, and he didn't know how else to attract our

86

The grotto at Schloss Linderhof, built deep in the hillside by King Ludwig II when Linderhof Castle was under construction.

Velvet settee on which Wagner died in the arms of his beloved wife Cosima at their Palazzo Vendramin in Venice. The following day Cosima had every piece of furniture burned except for this settee.

attention. A porter called for our luggage which had traveled in our private compartment with us, and we were soon in a taxi headed for our hotel. It proved to be a very elegant and modern one on the Opera Square just across the broad street from the Old University which Wagner had attended.

We started out by visiting the Old City Hall in the center of town. It was in this building that the man generally acknowledged to be Wagner's father worked as a minor police offical. The design of the building shows the Slavic influences in Leipzig, and its handsome clock-tower — topped by a copper dome now green with the patina of age — more closely resembles the style of the Czechs than that of the Saxon Germans.

A block away is the St. Thomas Church where Wagner studied organ and theory, and in whose parochial school he was enrolled for a time. This is the famous church where Johann Sebastian Bach was cantor for so many years. A huge stained-glass window now pays homage to this Baroque master; his grave occupies the center of the principal altar.

The Old University that Wagner attended is now only a roofless shell, a victim of World War II. Classic in design, it must have been a handsome building in its day. The Gewandhaus — that famous concert hall in which Wagner conducted — was also a ruin caused by the bombing raids. Whole sections of its facade have been destroyed and all of its interior is gutted. I was happy to note, however, that a marble bust of Mendelssohn has been placed on a column in front of the remains of the building, thus acknowledging once more after all the years of his ignominious neglect during Hitler's regime the existence of the man who did so much for the Gewandhaus concerts.

From Leipzig we drove out to Laustadt, about forty miles away. When Wagner was twenty-one he received his first important appointment as conductor for the Magdeburg Opera, which was then in residence at Laustadt. "This little watering place called Laustadt where the opera company was performing had, in the days of Goethe and Schiller, acquired a wide reputation. . . . Its wooden opera house had been built according to the design of the poet Goethe, and the first performance of several of his plays had been given in it."

Workmen were attempting to rehabilitate its interior when we arrived, in an effort to make the old theater usable again. Built entirely of wood, the opera house was small and unpretentious in appearance from the outside. After we had crawled through the scaffolding on our way inside, we caught a glimpse of an intimate theater. The stage is small, probably the proscenium opening no greater than twenty-five feet. The orchestra would probably seat 150 to 200, while the horseshoe-curved balcony could accommodate perhaps a hundred more. Classic columns of white wood framed the stage where Wagner conducted his first opera, Mozart's *Don Giovanni*. "Although I had never conducted before — certainly not an opera — the rehearsal and the performance came off fairly well."

BAVARIA AND SWITZERLAND

We headed south from Leipzig to Bayreuth and Munich, then on to Switzerland. To place things in a better chronological sequence, it would be wiser to discuss these areas in reverse order.

After Wagner became a political exile from Germany, he fled to Switzerland, settling in Zurich. This is surely one of the world's most attractive cities; a "beautiful spot," Wagner called it in his autobiography.

The Limmat River flows gently through this town, which is bordered on one side by the Alpine foothills and by the Lake of Zurich on the other. The spires of old churches rise from the rooftops on both sides of the river, the Romanesque Gross-Münster from the south and the Romanesque-Gothic Frau-münster on the north. The seventeenth-century city hall is right on the river bank. Colorful sailboats ply the lake, and a broad expanse of lawn and park circles the shore. The old Aktien-theater in Zurich, where in 1852 Wagner prepared and conducted a production of *The Flying Dutchman*, is gone, but most of the central part of the city must look today quite similar to the way it did then.

The Wessendonck Villa, where Richard and Minna Wagner once lived, is located in a large park on the northern slopes of the city. Now a museum of Chinese and Oriental art, it is beautifully preserved, looking quite serene in its setting among the trees. Large reflecting pools mirror the facade of the villa. Three gracefully curving arches rise the full height of this very tall two-storied home to frame its entrance hall. A stone balustrade bisects it at the level of the second floor.

Although the Wagners lived in a separate building, *Asyl* — a summer house — Richard spent much time at the Villa itself wooing Frau Wessendonck. It was this "friendship" that inspired *Tristan und Isolde* and led to the permanent separation of Richard and Minna.

After a visit to Venice, Wagner returned to Switzerland and lived in Lucerne for a brief time. Conducting the production of his operas occupied the next few years and led him to Paris, Vienna, and Russia. By this time his courtship of Cosima Liszt von Bülow was in full flower. In a moment of ardent passion he purchased a villa, Triebschen, a short distance from Lucerne. It was an idyllic setting: on a hill whose broad expanse of lawn sloped gracefully down to the edge of Lake Lucerne. Soon after occupying this villa, Richard and Cosima were married in the Protestant church of Lucerne. It was here at Triebschen that their son Siegfried was born. Today their former home is one of the most attractive Wagner museums.

Immediately inside the front door is the staircase leading to the second floor. It was on these steps that the composer placed his chamber orchestra on Christmas morning, 1870, to perform a surprise for his wife's birthday: his newly completed *Siegfried Idyll*.

The home today looks much like the description of it given by the French author, Judith Gautier, the daughter of the poet, who, in her book *Wagner At Home*, described her visit to Triebschen. She tells of the luxurious drawing room with "portraits of Beethoven, Goethe and Schiller upon the walls covered with rich yellow paper traced with arabesques in gold. . . . The gallery is a long, narrow room hung in violet velvet lined with small statues of Wagner's heroes and hung with pictures portraying scenes from *The Ring* and, in one corner, a butterfly collection and in another, a gilded Buddha, Chinese incense-burners, chisled cups and all sorts of rare and precious things."

Frau Gertrud Kappelar, the Curator of this Wagner museum, is a most charming woman who speaks excellent English in addition to French, German, and Italian. She made us feel right at home, and showed us many interesting and precious things in the collection. She pointed out to us the three silhouettes which Wagner carried with him everywhere. These silhouettes of Bach, Beethoven, and Weber — his three idols "of which Bach is the greatest" — hang on the opposite wall from the master's ornate grand piano which dominates the music room.

The main parlor, on the front side of the building with windows looking out across the lake, is now given over to museum display cases. The original score of the *Siegfried Idyll* is on exhibit, along with numerous photographs and daguerreotypes of the Wagner family, opera scores, playbills, and countless letters of Wagner and his artistic associates.

Two of the bedrooms upstairs now house a historical collection of instruments. Only one piano in the exhibit is Wagner's, the other spinets, viols, upright pianos, harps, etc., are part of an excellent collection of eighteenth and ninteenth-century musical instruments.

We left the house and followed the footpath down to the lake's edge. As we stood on its shore on a quiet, sunny July day, I was reminded of the description of the composer that Judith Gautier wrote as she found him standing there,

> "leaning both hands on the rough country fence, silent and with the earnest expression of concentration peculiar to him at times of internal emotion. His eyes, blue as the lake and almost motionless, seemed to be sucking the picture, from which a world of

ideas came streaming towards him. This place of refuge... made secure for him by the tenderness of the woman he loved at a time when he was most cruelly pursued by the bitter things of life; this lovely shrine, ... it was of this that he was thinking with such thankfulness."

MUNICH AND LUDWIG II

Wagner had not only been a political exile from Saxony in his youth, and thrown into debtor's prison during his residence in Paris; he was, in his fiftieth year, escaping creditors from Vienna where he had amassed enormous bills furnishing a sumptuous house for himself.

On a stopover in Munich, the composer became alarmed when, at a friend's house one evening, he was handed the calling card of no less a person than the private secretary to the King of Bavaria who wished to see him. Certain that the Austrian authorities had enlisted the aid of the Bavarian monarch, Wagner refused to see him. On returning to his hotel, he heard that the same gentleman had called there, too, and urgently desired to meet him. Wagner then arranged an interview for ten o'clock the following morning.

The King of Bavaria was a boy of nineteen, Ludwig II, who had just ascended to the throne. Wagner's music was the passion of his life, and when he read the composer's preface to the first edition of the *Ring* poem, he was taken with the paragraphs describing a great festival of the *Ring* which could be given if it could be financed by a benevolent prince. The preface ended with the words, "will such a prince appear?" Ludwig knew, as soon as he read this, that *he* was that prince.

Thus it was that at ten o'clock on the morning of May 3, 1864, the King's private secretary handed Wagner the monarch's signet ring and portrait, bidding him to come to the palace and meet the king. The composer reported that meeting in his autobiography:

"He wants me to stay with him always to work, to rest, to produce; he will give me all the money I need for that. I am to be my own abolute master, not a *kapellmeister*, nothing but myself and his friend......... What do you say to that? — What do you say? — Is it not fabulous? — Can it be anything but a dream?... My happiness is so great that I am quite overwhelmed by it."

A very strange relationship followed. True to his word, Ludwig paid all of the composer's considerable outstanding debts, furnished him with a large home in Munich, and eventually assisted with the building of the Festspielhaus and Wahnfried in Bayreuth.

At the time that Ludwig was helping the composer, he started on a building spree of his own, erecting two of the costliest castles in all of Europe, *Linderhof* and *Neuschwanstein*. As each was built, he had Wagner and his music dramas constantly in mind. Both palaces were decorated with scenes from various Wagnerian operas and, at Linderhof, a music room for Wagner's use was included in the plans.

No traveler to Europe should miss these showplaces of the "mad King" of Bavaria. They beggar description! They are exotic, ornate to the extreme, gaudy, fascinating, unbelievable.

Schloss Linderhof was begun in 1869 and started out to be a little garden chalet like Marly, at Versailles. Ludwig hired for an architect a stage designer named Christian Jank. When the castle was completed, it looked much more like a stage set than a place in which to live. It had only twelve rooms, excepting the servant's quarters, since the King had no queen and no children, never held any state dinners, balls, or receptions. He never invited anyone to spend the night, so he only needed one bedroom in each castle. Everything was designed especially for the place in which it stands, right down to the last towel rack and clothes hook. One wanders through room after room, completely dazzled by the splendor. There is a life-size porcelain peacock; an upright Aeolian piano covered with gold rococo squiggles is recognizable as a piano only on close inspection. (One wonders what Wagner thought as he played on it.) There is a canopy above the King's worktable lined with ermine from the coronation robe of his cousin, King Otto of Greece. Everything looks today as though it had just been put in place, for Ludwig and Wagner were the only persons that ever used the castle.

On the grounds of the Linderhof the King had an out-building called "Hundig's Hut" constructed. (It was destroyed during the war.) The hut was designed after the first act setting for *Die Walküre*, complete with a living ash tree in the middle pierced by a replica of Siegfried's sword. When the King was of the spirit, he would dress as an early Teuton and come to the hut for dinner, drinking mead out of an animal-horn cup. The salt and pepper shakers for the table were little owls, while a silver jug in the shape of a deer held the cream for his coffee. (What would Siegmund have said to that?)

Behind Linderhof a small footpath leads up the side of the hill. The trail seems to lead to a dead end, but by pressing a secret spring in a piece of papier-maché rock, a large slab of what appears to be rock swings open to reveal a grotto. We went inside to find ourselves in a room several hundred feet long and fifty feet high, hewn out of the rocky hillside. The guide told us that it wasn't rock at all, but brick and iron covered with canvas and cement to look like rocks and stalagmites. A good portion of the grotto is given over to an artificial lake in which the King used to swim; a waterfall gurgles noisily down from the bogus rocks, and, in Ludwig's day, rough waves on the lake could be generated by a small machine. He also had one of the first electric plants in Bavaria built here – twenty-five dynamos – so that the grotto could be lit by varicolored lights; a luminous rainbow was the most fantastic of his creations. In back of the lake a huge painting of Act I of *Tannhäuser* covers the wall. A gold and silver swan boat floats tranquilly on the lake. Ludwig once had the whole Munich opera company – orchestra, dancers, chorus, and soloists – brought to the grotto to perform the first act of that opera for an audience of one: Ludwig II!

Linderhof pales in comparison to Neuschwanstein, Ludwig's next project. He retained the same set designer as architect, and selected a craggy site with the Alps towering high above it and a green, fertile valley below. Although the King supervised the building of the castle, it took so long to complete that he only occupied it for six months.

The interior is not as pleasant to the eye as the exterior, for it is a horrible muddle of styles: Romanesque, Early Gothic, Late Gothic, Tudor, Moorish, and Byzantine. The walls are covered with frescos and paintings of the great Wagner characters: Tristan and Isolde, Lohengrin and Elsa, Walther and Eva. In the King's study there is a painting of the Venusberg scene from Tannhäuser (what *was* the King's fascination with this scene?); a bored-looking Tannhäuser, fully clothed, sits at Venus's feet gazing the other way. Venus, completely naked, looks no more sensual in spite of her nudity than Whistler's mother fully clothed.

But if Ludwig's fairy-tale castles proved to be of little practical value, Wagner's building spree led to two structures built for posterity, the *Festspielhaus* and *Roman Wahnfried*.

BAYREUTH

Wagner originally went to Bayreuth because he had heard that its Court Theater had the largest stage in Germany. Erected during the years 1745 to 1748 on a design by Galli Bibiena, the Margrave's opera house is today one of the most elegant theaters in Europe. As Wagner discovered, it is essentially a small theater, seating perhaps a hundred in its series of regal boxes of white, each gilded with gold rococo swirls. The orchestra — a beautiful parquet floor — will accommodate perhaps 150 to 200 folding chairs. The proscenium is covered by gold cherubs and angels so dear to the heart of the rococo decorators. Unfortunately the stage was much too small for Wagner's vast Teutonic music sagas.

The Margrave's *Residenz*, the former seat of the court, is still in the center of town. It was here that Wagner called on the

95

Margrave and talked of building his own opera house. One wing of the Residenz is now given over to a Wagner museum filled with priceless heirlooms donated by the Wagner family. One room which appears to be a study contains the master's desk and the piano that he used at Wahnfried. Scenic sketches of all the productions at the Festspielhaus, from 1876 to the present season, are framed and hang on the walls. In one room stands the little love-seat, covered in maroon velvet (now almost threadbare) on which the composer died in the arms of his wife. It was the only piece of furniture that Cosima preserved from their home in Venice after he passed away; she had all the other furniture destroyed.

Many manuscripts, printed editions, and playbills of his music dramas appear in locked cases. All the principal portraits of the composer, either originals or excellent copies, are to be found here. There are two wonderful paintings of Cosima elaborately framed, and a portrait of Richard's brother Albert. The resemblance between the two brothers is striking! The self-portrait of Ludwig Geyer, Wagner's stepfather, also hangs in this museum.

The *Festspielhaus* stands high on a hill overlooking Bayreuth. It was about a twenty- minute walk up a tree-shaded lane from our hotel to the opera house. Broad parks with fountains and fish ponds line this avenue as it approaches the Festspielhaus. The front of the opera house, slightly damaged during the war, has been restored so that it looks exactly the same as it does in the photographs taken in the 1880's. The interior remains as Wagner designed it, largely constructed of wood which gives the house a unique resonance and excellent acoustics. And, of course, it has its famed "hidden" orchestra pit.

The backside of the building, which includes the stage and dressing rooms, has been enlarged considerably. These renovations and additions do not show from the front and therefore do not disturb one's image of Wagner's theater. Behind the opera house is a workshop where sets are built, properties and drops stored, and the mechanical devices for the stage made ready. A restaurant has been built on the east side of the Festspielhaus.

It was great fun to ramble on a summer morning among this complex of buildings, listening to the orchestra rehearse in the restaurant as the singers went through a piano rehearsal on stage. Workmen in the shop were making ready the tree for the first act of *Die Walküre*.

Back in the center of town, off to the side behind the Residenz, stands *Wahnfried*, the home financed largely by Ludwig and designed by Wagner. "Here where my illusions have found peace," the composer wrote to his King, "I have built my home and called it 'peace from illusion — *Wahnfried*,'" The name Wahnfried comes from that of an old village in Germany. "That name has always had a mystical effect on me," Wagner confided.

Siegfried Wagner's widow, Winifred — the great friend of Adolph Hitler — still lives at Wahnfried, along with her remaining son, Wolfgang, and his family. Because of this, the front yard is open for tourists to wander about, but the house itself is closed to the public. There is nothing left inside, anyway, of the composer's furnishings and belongings; they have all been donated to the Museum where they are on permanent display. The garden side of Wahnfried was seriously damaged during the War, but it is now completely restored.

The building is strange in its architecture, for it looks much more like a municipal building than a private residence. The two-storied red sandstone structure has no visible roof. Classic columns with a pediment frame and main entrance; a large fresco about 16 by 30 feet is painted above the doorway. The circular carriage drive is built around a bronze bust on a pedestal of Ludwig II who made all this possible.

From the park side of the home, one can visit the master's grave. Bowers of trees arch over it; thick shrubs and neatly trimmed ivy surround it. At Wagner's wish, there is no inscription on the flat tombstone, for all the world must surely know that here is the grave of Richard Wagner.

There is an inscription on a very small tombstone a few feet away, for it is the grave of the master's pet dog. *His* name and dates are inscribed on the marble as Wagner wished it to be.

The building in which Giacomo Puccini was born, 30 via di Poggia, in Lucca, stands at the left. The Puccini apartment was on the second floor.

Conservatory of Music in Lucca attended by Puccini as a young man. Known in his day as the *Pacini Institute*, the name was later changed to honor one of Lucca's more prominent composers, Luigi Boccherini.

VII
PUCCINI: SPORTSMAN AND COMPOSER

The aged city of Lucca lies near the Serchio River whose headwaters are in the imposing Tuscan hills that form a backdrop for the city. It was founded by the Romans who, in the sixth century, built a broad, protective wall completely around the town. Lucca prospered and became famous for its velvets and damasks, and, in the twelfth century, a medièval banking center. Its artistic zenith was reached by the fifteenth century with the completion of the churches of San Michele and San Frediano.

We first approached Lucca from the south, having driven up from Florence. It was early on a warm, sunny morning in July. Our first glimpse was of the broad parkway of green grass and shade trees that surround the ancient Roman wall which still majestically encircles the inner city; above the top of this fortification we could see the spires and belfries of Lucca's many churches. As we got out of our rented Fiat convertible to take some photographs, we noticed other automobiles driving around on top of the wall. We discovered that the old barrier now provides a most propitious vantage point from which to see the city without ever leaving one's car!

We approached the western gate in the wall and quickly drove into the heart of the city. We found a place to park the car and started off on foot. We immediately made a most pleasant discovery: there were practically no tourists in Lucca even though it was then the height of the season. What a relief not to have to bump into camera- and binocular-laden families, the husband dressed in ridiculous-looking walking shorts, brightly colored sportshirt and Babe Ruth baseball cap, accompanied by a hefty wife attired in tight-fitting slacks (too much pasta en route?), drip-dry blouse, the whole surmounted by a bright bandana that might be an attempt to camouflage some hair-rollers. Apparently the American travel agencies had booked their clients on a Rome — Florence — Pisa route, missing Lucca because it lacked a Colosseum or *David* by Michelangelo or leaning tower. In place of tourists, we found the sidewalks filled with the local citizens, cheerful, friendly Tuscans who were most courteous and interested in seeing that we enjoyed our visit to their city.

All the streets in the old part of town are quite narrow; three or four-story buildings rise immediately from the sidewalks edge on both sides. We found the Via de Poggio and hunted for No. 30, the apartment house in which Giacomo Puccini had been born on December 22, 1858. We located it easily, for a plaque honoring the composer is now attached to the wall. (It was placed there exactly one month after his death in 1924.) The brick and stone building has a red tile roof; graceful arches top the windows and central doorway on the ground floor, while green wooden shutters frame the rectangular windows of the upper two floors.

The Puccinis had occupied the apartment on the second floor. Nothing remains of their furnishings, though, for when Giacomo was five his father died, leaving Albina Puccini to rear Giacomo, his younger brother and five sisters on a widow's pension. She had to auction off most of the family's possessions to support her children.

Just down the Via de Poggio is the dazzling and beautiful church of San Michele with its tall, light, and graceful facade of countless white marble columns standing in rows on top of more white marble columns in rows. A short distance away is the church of San Paolino, the parish church where Giacomo first studied the pipe organ. All his forebears had been organists, and his late father's position at the eleventh-century cathedral of San Martino was filled by his uncle only until Giacomo himself became of an age and had the technical proficiency necessary to fill the position.

It is a known fact that as a lad Giacomo was mischievous and full of pranks. His parish priest later told a tale about

100

Giacomo and one of his companions, a story repeated by Puccini himself many times in later life. Giacomo and his friend presented themselves to the sexton at one of the churches, requesting permission to practise the pipe organ. "And do you know what the rascals did?" wrote the priest. "While they took turns pretending to practise, they removed some of the organ pipes and sold them so they could buy candy and cigarettes!"

Giacomo's Uncle Magi, who had attempted to give the boy lessons in singing and pipe organ, finally gave up. Speaking in a typically Italian proverb, he told Albina Puccini, "Your son is meat which does not wish to be salted." He told the widow that her son had no *talento* and called him *Giacomo Puccini-falento* — "Giacomo, Slow-learner Puccini."

In desperation Albina Puccini went to see a friend of hers at the Conservatory, Carlo Angeloni, a young teacher who had been a pupil of her husband. She implored him to enroll Giacomo at the music school; he agreed.

We walked the dozen or so blocks across town to the conservatory. In Puccini's day it had been called the Pacini Institute, but the school was re-named in 1943 in honor of the two-hundredth anniversary of another renowned native musician. It is now known as the *Instituto Musicale Luigi Boccherini*. The conservatory is near the Eastern Porta Elisa and is protected from the noise of the streets by a high wall. We entered through its central arch, reminiscent of the arches of the Roman forum, and immediately found ourselves in a pleasant garden courtyard. The two-storied stucco building of the school, built not too long before Giacomo first enrolled, is a U-shaped structure. An alabaster bust of Boccherini now occupies the center of the long, narrow courtyard filled with orange trees, flowers, and shrubs. It was here, under the teaching of Carlo Angeloni, that the spark of genius in young Giacomo first took hold. Soon the boy was an enthusiastic pupil.

In order to help with the expenses at home, Puccini now sought out a job at night playing for a local café, "Il Buon Gusto." His pay was the equivalent of a dollar a night plus all the pastry he could eat. (He later held similar jobs at the casino and the pavillion.) Today the café, located in Via Mordini, is called "Café Fanciulla della West" in honor of the illustrious piano-player of a hundred years ago.

One autumn day in 1880, when Puccini was almost twenty-two, he left Lucca. He had his certificate of graduation from the Pacini Institute and headed for Milan to further his musical studies. Like Verdi before him, the young Puccini spent a number of years in Milan studying and arranging for the productions of his first operas, *Le Villi* (at the Teatro dal Verme which is now a movie theater) and *Edgar* (at La Scala). As soon as he was artistically and financially secure, he returned to the region of his birth. *Manon Lescaut* was the turning point.

TORRE DEL LAGO

Puccini selected a spot for his home just twenty miles from Lucca, a fishing village of about 120 inhabitants called *Torre del Lago* — "Tower of the Lake." It was located on the western shore of Lake Massaciucoli, between Viareggio and Pisa. The shallow lake is not too large; dark green mountains surround it. A pine forest stretches for miles around the water which itself is overgrown with reeds and rushes. The composer chose this location for three reasons: it was not a well-know location, therefore a house could be rented (and later purchased) quite cheaply; it was inaccessible, therefore affording privacy; and it was an ideal spot for hunting and fishing. Puccini considered this his home from 1891 until 1921, and all his operas from *La Boheme* onward, with the exception of *Turandot*, were completed in Torre. The original residence of Giacomo and Elvira, who was later to become Mrs. Puccini, was in the stone tower that had given the village its name; later the composer had it razed and built his own home as the tower was much too cold and damp in winter.

Puccini had referred to Torre del Lago as "my supreme joy, paradise, Eden, the Empyrean, *turris eburnea, vas spirituale*, and kingdom." Unfortunately I had expected to find his beloved Torre much as he left it. What a disappointment!

Lake Massaciucoli, half-way between Lucca and Viareggio on the sea coast. When Puccini moved there in 1889 the area was inhabited by only a few hearty fishermen who lived in little huts.

Torre del Lago, literally "Tower of the Lake," was an old stone tower Puccini purchased in which to live. He tore it down and built this Mediterranean style home in its place.

Resort cottages, of the cheapest and most garish sort, line every road and street for miles around the western shore of the lake. Where once the waters of the lake brushed closely by the entrance to Puccini's villa, allowing the composer to slip easily into a boat and head out on one of his hunting expeditions, a quay has now been built. A Coney-Island type of restaurant is located on the quay, blocking the villa's view of the lake. In the area between the Puccini home and the restaurant there are half a dozen stands at which post cards are for sale, cheap plaster busts of the composer may be purchased, all in addition to the trivia sold in any cheap seaside resort.

An iron fence separates the villa and garden from the busy throng of tourists that now frequent the quay. A caretaker unlocked the gate to admit us to the grounds; the villa now belongs to Rita Puccini, the composer's daughter-in-law. The two-story home, of light ochre-colored stucco, is of typical Mediterranean design. Palm trees and flower beds are to be found in the little garden in front of the house.

Several photographs were taken during the composer's lifetime inside the villa. In comparing these old pictures with what we saw, we were pleased to discover that the rooms have been restored as faithfully as possible. One enters the music room first, a parlor dominated by the composer's old upright Forester piano.

The ceiling is beamed; rich scroll work and painted geometric designs cover each one. The recessed squares of the ceiling are alternately green and maroon, each with a gold medallion in the center. The walls are relatively plain, but the doorways are capped with ornate arches of gold sculptured bas relief. The windows are of translucent bottle-glass, the inside wooden shutters painted in intricate geometric patterns of pink, yellow-green, powder blue, and gold.

An old oak swivel chair sits in front of the piano, a writing table immediately to its left. Brackets on either side of the piano's music rack hold pairs of candles. The top of the instrument is covered with framed pictures, among which one of Elvira Puccini and one of their son Tonio are prominent.

Puccini's study at Torre del Lago is ornately decorated. His old upright Forester piano (on which most of *Boheme, Butterfly* and *Tosca* were composed) is covered with portraits of singers and conductors.

Wilderness retreat in the Tuscan Hills at Montsegrati was only one of Puccini's investments in high-mountain homes.

Across the room is a felt-covered writing table with an elaborate gold pen-and-ink stand of Baroque flavor. Overstuffed chairs are to be found on either side of the table.

If the music room is over-decorated and cluttered, it is mild compared to the study! Again the ceiling is ornate, deep panels painted in shades of brown and maroon are separated by beams trimmed with busy little patterns. A three-foot band caps the plain walls just under the ceiling; plaster cherubs are sculptured into this band at frequent intervals. Green garlands in the della Robbia style, with peaches, pears, and apples interwoven, link the cherubs. Several panels covered with colorful frescos of classical design appear in the walls about the room. The furnishings are all of dark-stained, almost black, oak. Portraits, busts, and photographs abound. A photograph of Geraldine Farrar as Butterfly is the most prominent; a picture of Puccini's librettist Luigi Illica hangs nearby. A bust of Dante Alighieri reposes on the music cabinet. Various laurel wreaths, trophies, and awards presented to the composer during his lifetime are hung over the carved oak fireplace mantel.

In one of the side rooms all the maestro's guns and firearms are kept, reminders of his great love of hunting. His rain slicker hangs on a rack on the wall while his hip boots are nearby. The story is told that one day Puccini and two friends sped across the lake in the maestro's speedboat, "Mimi I," because the hunting looked better on that side. Although Puccini had purchased all the hunting rights on his side of the lake, he was headed for the shore where he thought the game birds would be. The trio were arrested on the triple charge of shooting out of season, trespassing on private property, and possessing firearms without a permit!

THE TUSCAN HILLS

Throughout his life, Puccini searched for wild mountain retreats in the Tuscan hills, as far away from civilization and people as he could get. Elvira hated these places and thought Giacomo was foolish to invest his money in the purchase of them.

106

Searching out these secluded homes led us onto roads over which few automobiles have probably passed since Puccini drove his 1903 Clement motorcar over them. The countryside, even now, is remote and rustic. The sky has a clear splendor, and at dawn and dusk a delicate vapor rises from the earth, softening the outline of tree and hill, bathing them in muted colors. The hillsides are covered with vegetation: olives silvering over so many slopes; the vine — producer of so many famous wines — growing in close lines as far as they eye can see; flowers in profusion in splendid little family gardens; and the ambivalent cypress giving elegance and character to every outlined horizon.

We first visited the hamlet of Monsegrati where Puccini had purchased a home in which to work on *Tosca*. Although the map showed the village to be only fifteen km (about ten miles) from Lucca, it took almost thirty minutes to drive the last three miles. The dirt road is narrow, even for a little Fiat, steep and full of chuck holes. It climbs swiftly and is made up of one switch-back after another. Eventually we reached Monsegrati, a village of perhaps half a dozen homes perched on a flat mountain top about twelve hundred feet above sea level. All the houses, Puccini's included, are built of stone, some using the "dry wall" technique, others cemented together with mortar. Crude, hand-hewn beams support the flat roofs, and doors and window frames are cut out of the roughest lumber. The villagers cautiously peeked out to see the modern automobile that had invaded their hamlet, and to learn who might be in it. I'm certain that most of them had never seen an American, let alone two of them.

The loneliness of this hidden village reminded me of the maestro's contradictory description of it in a letter which he wrote to his publisher. He said, "I am in a hideous, hateful place, drowned in the middle of trees and woods so that one can see nothing. I am shut in by the mountains and lighted by the boiling sun. Hot! Hot! Hot! I sleep by day and work at night, because the evenings are delicious and the nights enchanting. I work from ten at night to four in the morning. I am happy to be here where human beings are exceptions. I am really alone!"

As we retraced our steps down the treacherously narrow, winding road, it was very easy to envision how Puccini had overturned his primitive 1906 automobile while racing downhill. The accident nearly cost him his life (he was pinned under the vehicle). As it was, he was bedridden for eight months with two broken legs, and then confined to a wheelchair after that.

While working on *Madama Butterfly*, Puccini decided to become a recluse in Abetone. Lying at an elevation of 5000 feet and more then seventy miles from Lucca, it was quite a drive! Today Abetone is one of the famous winter ski resorts of Italy and a vacation center in summer, so the roadway, while steep and winding, was paved and permitted travel in both directions. The home Puccini occupied while working on *Butterfly* is now a small hotel, "Lo Scoglietto" — "the Little Rock." An apt name, since it is perched on the side of the hill and is built of brick-shaped rock. The building looks like a medieval fortress. A square tower overlooks the deep valley below; a roofed loggia, now a restaurant, extends across the width of the building over its second floor. Bright red window shutters stand out in strong contrast to the natural rock color of the walls.

Today Abetone is a typical resort town. There are more than thirty hotels of various sizes and classes, a dozen restaurants, first aid stations (for the benefit of skiers in winter), and two Catholic churches. Although Abetone is not a spot frequented by Americans, it was filled with camping and sport enthusiasts from all over Germany and Italy.

To find the little village of Chiatri was much more fun, for this was and is the most isolated of all the Puccini mountain retreats. Located halfway between Lucca and Torre del Lago, it lies miles back into the Tuscan hills. The composer picked this spot after returning from his first successful American visit to the Metropolitan Opera House in New York; it was at Chiatri that he was going to commence work on his "American" opera — *The Girl of the Golden West*.

108

Puccini's home at Viareggio served the Maestro after the fumes at Torre del Lago forced him to move. All of his work on *Turandot* was done in this house.

Ste. Mariakerk in Brussels, located in what used to be the Italian district of the city. Here the first funeral service was held for Puccini.

109

I couldn't help but wonder how much the creation of the opera, its libretto and stage decor, was influenced by this tiny hamlet. Certainly the California mining town in which the action of the opera takes place must have resembled, in Puccini's mind, the village of Chiatri. Olive trees and grape vineyards cover the rolling hills; the merciless sun beats down with intense heat. Isolated by miles of sinuous roads from the closest town, life is, at best, primitive. Only the building materials differed. Where the shacks of a California mining town might have been constructed out of native lumber (although I have seen a number of stone buildings in the Mother Lode country) the few homes in Chiatri were built of stone and rock chinked with a crude form of mortar.

Asked why he picked such an inaccessible spot in which to compose. Puccini replied that he "liked to be far away for the sake of work. An invitation to dinner makes me sick for a week. I wasn't born for a life of drawing rooms and parties. I love the wild country too much."

VIAREGGIO AND TURANDOT

During World War I Puccini was confined to his home at Torre del Lago due to the exigencies of the war and because a gasoline shortage kept him from motoring. *La Rondine* and his Triptych —'*Gianni Schichi, Il Tabarro* and *Suor Angelica* — were completed within these years.

No sooner was the Armistice signed than a peat factory was built up the lake from Puccini's villa. The stench from the bogs which they were opening up made life absolutely unbearable for the composer. Reluctantly he left Torre and moved to Viareggio, a seaside community about ten miles to the west on the Levantian Riviera of the Ligurian Sea.

He purchased a home about two blocks from the water's edge, a rambling structure that faced a beautiful pine forest. The Puccini villa is an impressive, almost palatial building, but rather somber and uninviting. It is built of red brick, with a gabled roof under which runs a relief showing ancient Greek masks and lyres. Wide steps lead up to a large veranda which is shaded by pine and olive trees.

Although Viareggio has built up over the years, the pine forest across the street from the former Puccini home has been preserved as a park. The villa is now occupied as a commercial residence, and nothing of the composer's furnishings remain.

It was while living at Viareggio that Puccini learned from his doctors that he had cancer of the throat. They told him that the only hope for recovery was to undergo the then new radium treatment. Puccini packed his incomplete score of *Turandot* and prepared to go to L'Institut de la Couronne in Brussels where such radium treatments could be given.

Rain was pelting down on the cobblestone streets of Brussels the day we searched for the Institut de la Couronne. The institute is now the Hôspital Militaire de Bruxelles located at number 145 on the Avenue de la Couronne. A more drab and dismal looking building would be hard to imagine. The hospital is a large, rambling two-storied structure some several hundred feet in length; the age-darkened sandstone facade makes it appear much more like a prison than a hospital. The painted white frames of its tiny windows stand out in great contrast to the depressing appearance of the fortress-like structure.

Just when the radium treatments seemed to be taking effect, Puccini's heart gave way. After a good day, around six p.m. in the evening, the composer slumped in his chair. He never rallied. Around 4 a.m. the next morning he passed away.

The first funeral service was conducted December 1, 1924, in Brussels at the Ste. Mariakerk, Schaarbeek, a parish church in the Italian quarter of the city. It is a beautiful old edifice that sits in the center of a traffic circle formed by the intersection of six streets. A huge copper dome, now green with the patina of age, towers above the tall walls of this intimate, yet impressive church. A Brussels newspaper, in a story dated about a month after we had visited Ste. Marie, announced that the church was being torn down so that a freeway interchange could be built to accommodate the major streets that intersect at that point; a tall hotel-office building was then to be erected over it and the parish church relocated elsewhere. Apparently the newspaper story served its purpose; the Belgians strongly objected to the possible loss of this shrine, and other freeway plans are now being made.

After the service at the church of Ste. Marie, the composer's body was transported to Milan where a memorial service was conducted on December 3. All Italy was in public mourning. Flags flew at half staff. La Scala was closed. In the magnificent Milan cathedral Arturo Toscanini conducted the Requiem music from Puccini's early opera *Edgar*.

The composer's body was buried first in the Toscanini family plot, and then later removed to Torre del Lago to be enshrined in the wall of his home in a special mausoleum that his son Tonio had constructed there.

VIII
DEBUSSY: MUSICIEN FRANÇAIS

Strangely elusive in France is the spirit of Claude Debussy, the composer who signed his last works with the proud, simple signature: *Claude Debussy, musicien français.* All that remains is a series of addresses of where he once lived. Nothing more, nothing less. It is almost as though Debussy, both as a man and as an artist, never existed.

Paris was not only Debussy's abode for most of his life, it was always his spiritual home. Today Paris is unable to conjure anything that recalls that master of music!

Our search began at St. Germain-en-Laye, the little suburb of Paris in which Claude Debussy was born on August 22, 1862. The village is about a half-hour's taxi ride from central Paris, and we headed northwest out of town. St. Germain sits on a ridge above a large bend in the Seine, and as we approached it the high Château that dominates the town came into view. This ancient castle was started by Louis VI in the twelfth century. Its surrounding moats were once filled with water; the main building, an irregular pentagon, has a flat roof edged with vases in classic design.

The royal court used the Château as a residence from the time of its construction until Louis XIV had Versailles built in 1682. It was at the Château that Mary Stuart lived from the age of six to sixteen before her marriage with the Dauphin, Francis; here that James II of England — James Stuart — ended his days after being deposed.

Just two blocks up the street from the Château is Rue au Pain — "Bread Street." We turned left and walked for two more blocks to No. 38. In this old building Manuel Achille Debussy once ran a china and porcelain shop. He rented an apartment above his store to house his family, and it was in one of its rooms that his son was born. He named the boy Achille-Claude.

113

(Years later the son chose to reverse the order of his given names.) Within two years after Achille-Claude's birth, the china shop went bankrupt and the family moved to Paris.

Today the Rue au Pain is a business thoroughfare as it has been for more than 200 years. There is nothing in particular to characterize it, for it resembles thousands of similar middle-class shopping districts. The Château a few blocks away has nothing to do with this urban center of everyday life and activity. It is a narrow, noisy, and busy street. Shoppers crowd the sidewalks, stopping at tobacco shops, or bakeries, or clothiers. Today, at No. 38, the ground floor houses a cleaning and dyeing establishment. Above its sign is a tablet announcing this spot as the birthplace of the composer. The plaque was placed there by a group of English admirers five years after Debussy's death. A worn and scarred wooden staircase leads upstairs from a dingy vestibule and court to the former Debussy living quarters.

Achille-Claude must have been christened just before the family moved from St. Germain, as he was approaching two years of age at the time of the ceremony. It took place in the Church of St. Germain-en-Laye which stands just across the large square from the Château. It is a simple, but not unimposing structure, built in 1827 of a neo-classical design. The portico, with its six huge pillars supporting a lofty frieze, tends to dwarf the church behind it.

We headed back for central Paris, intending to visit a series of addresses that we had. It seems that Debussy's father was a ne'er-do-well and changed jobs and residences almost once every twelve months for the first few years after he lost the china shop. First he was a traveling salesman, next a printer's assistant, then a soldier in the guard during the Commune uprising. The Debussys lived first at 11 Rue Vintimille, a large apartment building similar to many others built during Haussmann's reconstruction of Paris in the middle of the nineteenth century. It has a five-story sandstone facade rising immediately from the sidewalk's edge. Shops and stores occupy the ground floor; large apartments with balconied windows appear immediately above. The roof is sloped, the gables of the attic

114

Rue au Pain ("Bread Street") in St. Germain-en-Laye was named for the bakers that once plied their trade here. At the time of Debussy's birth the street had become one of countless little first floor shops with living apartments above them.

The apartment in which Claude Debussy was born, at 38 Rue au Pain, was two floors above his father's china shop. Manuel Debussy, originally from Burgundy, moved to this apartment after his marriage.

apartments projecting towards the street. Tall smoke stacks with chimney pots on top — those familiar landmarks which give the Paris skyline its character — abound on the roof. A double door of golden oak opens onto a small hallway; a stairway leads to the upper floors. While the Debussys lived here Claude's mother took in sewing to augment her husband's meager income as a traveling salesman in household goods.

Manual Debussy became a lithographer's assistant after losing his job as a salesman. The family moved to 68 Rue St. Honoré, a less fashionable apartment house. The building is narrow; only one small store occupies the ground floor. Each of the three apartments — one to a floor — has two windows opening on the street and small windows facing the courtyard at the back of the building.

Manuel Debussy was no more successful as a printer than he had been at his other occupations. After losing this position, he moved his family into his father's home at 3 Impasse de l'Ecole. From there the family moved to their own home at 59bis Rue Pigalle, occupying an apartment there while Manuel Debussy served in he army during the Commune uprising of March, 1871. The apartment house in the Rue Pigalle greatly resembles the earlier one on Rue Vintimille: sandstone facade, balconied first floor, gabled roof with chimney pots. Paris has hundreds of apartment houses just like it.

Achille-Claude was enrolled at the Paris Conservatory when he was twelve years old. His tuition was paid by the government and his living expenses at home were borne by his father who harbored visions of his son becoming a prosperous piano virtuoso. During these early days at the Conservatory, the family moved still another time, on this occasion to a humble fourth-floor flat in Rue Clapeyron. Manuel Debussy was now a bookkeeper!

By the time Achille-Claude was seventeen, he decided to seek summer employment in order to earn a little pocket money. His piano teacher at the Conservatory recommended him for a chamber music group hired each summer by Mme.

116

Marguerite Wilson-Pelouze to play at her château of Chenonceaux.

One of Debussy's biographers, Edward Lockspeiser, has remarked that "the few months that the seventeen-year-old student spent at the historic château in the Touraine has hardly been mentioned in any of the biographies. . . . I do not think we can over-rate this early experience. Responsive to the luxury of physical surroundings, the impecunious youth, insecure in his family environment in the rue Clapeyron, must have been overwhelmed by the magnificence of the former residence of Diane de Poitiers and Catherine de' Medici."[1]

Chenonceaux is located on the River Cher whose headwaters are near St. Amand-Montrond and the Canal du Berry. The fertile valley formed by it and the Loire (which it joins at Tours) is known as the Garden of France. The river is broad, its flow gentle. The surface is frequently like that of a mirror, reflecting the luminous clouds that float through a clear blue sky, serene as the river itself. During the Middle Ages, the first fortresses were erected along the banks of these two rivers: Angers, Chinon, Langeais, and Loches. They were massive, stark, and grim. More harmonious with the landscape, more typical of the Val du Loire, are the châteaux of a later age, built by French kings home from the Italian wars and dazzled by new visions of *la douceur de vivre.*

We approached Chenonceaux through a magnificent arch of planes, huge trees which had been planted by Diane de Poitiers. The château, which quickly came into view, was built by Henri II as a gift for her, his mistress. Diane, in turn, commissioned the brilliant architect Philibert Delorme to build the stunning bridge which joins the castle to the left bank of the Cher. On the death of Henri II, his wife, Catherine de' Medici, seized the chateau and had two stories added to the bridge. Today Chenonceaux and the bridge are reflected in the clear, still water of the Cher.

One wonders what the seventeen-year-old Claude felt when

[1] Lockspeiser, Edward. *Debussy: His Life and Mind.* New York: The Macmillan Company, 1962 (volume 1)

he first beheld this Renaissance jewel: the graceful arches of the bridge, the round turrets of the château proper, the gabled roof of slate with tall, stately chimneys, the exquisite formal gardens. The interior of the chateau is even more breathtaking! The ceilings alone are phenomenal in their beauty and detail; rich tapestries and textured papers cover the walls. Deeply carved Renaissance furniture, heavy yet graceful, decorate the rooms; oil paintings of the masters, in handsome gilded frames, grace the walls. Certainly this opened up new avenues of beauty for Debussy and enlarged his aesthetic experience.

Once summer was over, Claude was back at work at the Conservatory. The following vacation he was hired by Nadejda von Meck, the great patroness of Tchaikovsky, who employed Debussy as a pianist for her trio. The young man then had a chance of visiting her summer homes in Russia, in Italy, and in Switzerland.

During the fall and winter months, Debussy tried for the Prix de Rome at the Conservatory. Finally his cantata, *The Prodigal Son*, was accepted for consideration. The final judging was to take place at the Palais d'Institut, the home of the Académie des Beaux-Arts which sponsored the prize. The Palais is located on Rue Conti on the Left Bank, just across the Seine from the Louvre. It is one of the most handsome and graceful buildings in the world's most handsome and graceful city. It was built in the seventeenth century by Cardinal Mazarin and has been used since 1806 for the meetings of the Academy. Of neo-classical design, a broad portico sweeps around in a half circle. Huge pillars support the central frieze; the building behind it is capped by a dome of black slate decorated with brightly shining gold ribs and surmounted by a golden cupola.

In the rotunda underneath the dome, the Prix de Rome contest was held. The interior of the Palais is as impressive as its exterior. Tall marble columns support round, Romanesque arches above which the dome is surmounted. The floor is a mosaic of highly colored and intricate design. Niches for statuary groupings surround the rotunda; bas reliefs appear above each niche.

The Debussys' home on Rue St. Honoré, in the little apartment two floors above the *Chez Jean* sign. It was one of many in which Claude lived as a youth.

Claude Debussy's apartment on Rue Cardinet is the only apartment of Debussy in Paris marked by a plaque. This one was erected by English friends of the composer.

Needless to say, Debussy won the contest with *The Prodigal Son* and was awarded three years of study at the French Academy in Rome.

ROME AND THE RETURN TO PARIS

The French Academy in Rome occupies the historic Villa Medici, located in the Borghese Park. These gardens were designed in the sixteenth century by Cardinal Scipione; it is the largest park in Rome with a perimeter of some 3½ miles. Its southern border touches Trinità dei Monti where Charles VIII of France had a magnificent Baroque church erected. Adjoining the church is the Villa Medici, built in the second half of the sixteenth century to a design by Annibale Lippi. The Villa dominates the Trinità dei Monti; it has a view of Rome which stretches from the Campidoglio to St. Peter's Basilica. The fountain in front is simple: a large concrete bowl in the center of which is the cannon ball which Queen Christina of Sweden had fired from a mortar on the Castle Sant'Angelo during her stay in Rome.

The ornate Renaissance facade of the Villa Medici faces the Borghese Gardens. The design is a plethora of architectural devices – arches, columns, niches, statuary, friezes, towers, loggias and balustrades.

Debussy was not happy at the Villa. "My life as a student here at the Villa," the composer wrote home, "is a life that has something in common with the life of a cosmopolitan hotel. I can tell now that my first impressions were not very favorable. The other students are so egotistical. Their converations very much resemble gossip at a café, and it would be idle to imagine that new theories of art could evolve here. . . . As I walked through the doorway of the Villa, the thought occurred to me that this was the home of mediocre art. I have tried to work, but have not been able to. This just isn't the place for me. It isn't pride that makes me hate the life, it is that I simply cannot get used to it."

Before his three years were up, Debussy quit the Academy in disgust and returned to his beloved Paris. "I could no longer drag out a monstrous, easy life. In Rome, I could come to nothing, my mind was dead."

On moving back to Paris, Debussy went to live with a friend of his, a wealthy financier and patron of music named Etienne Dupin who lived at 76 Rue des Malesherbes. The composer must have felt at home, for he was once again living in an apartment building designed and built during the Haussmann reconstruction of Paris. It resembled two of his earlier homes, the one on Rue Vintimille and the Rue Pigalle residence.

We decided that we must look elsewhere than at residences if we were going to find anything of significance in our Debussy pilgrimage. We turned to the most obvious tourist delights of the city, for it was in these very places that the *musicien français* found inspiration.

In formulating his musical style, Debussy was deeply impressed by the Paris World Exhibition of 1889. To celebrate this centennial of the French Revolution, a huge steel tower was erected on the Champs des Mars. In addition to Gustave Eiffel's great feat of engineering, the Exhibition included many exotic displays from the near and far east. The pavilions of China and the Dutch East Indies included performances. These eastern influences were later reflected in such compositions as the *Quartet* with its suggestion of the Javanese gamelang, and in *Pagodas* for piano based on the pentatonic scale which hints of the Oriental aspect with "shimmering gold surfaces, feline grace of dancers and people, the infinite fixation underlying the surface barocity of noises" (according to E. Robert Schmitz).[1]

The great Paris Metro — the subway system — was constructed for the World Exhibition. Each terminal or station was designed in the *art nouveau* style, with great swirling wrought iron balustrades in peacock and flower designs. These arabesques of metal are not too far removed in spirit from the *Arabesques* for piano which Debussy composed.

[1] Schmitz, E. Robert. *The Piano Works of Claude Debussy.* New York: Duell, Sloan & Pearce, Inc., 1950

The cafés of Montmartre were a favorite haunt of Debussy and his colleagues — poets, authors, painters, and musicians. At the Tavern Weber he met the famous writer Marcel Proust, while at Reynolds he became acquainted with Henri de Toulouse-Lautrec, the crippled artist. Toulouse-Lautrec painted many portraits of Parisian clowns which, in turn, inspired several of Debussy's compositions: *Minstrels,* the *Golliwog's Cake-Walk* and parts of *The Toy Box.* Many of Debussy's songs were settings of texts written by his café friends Mallarmé and Verlaine.

Today Montmartre retains much of the flavor and decor of the 1890's, buried as it is on the side of the hill adjoining *Sacre Coeur* which caps the mountain. But one must be selective in choosing a time to visit the area if the intention is to recapture the earlier spirit, for Montmartre is both a traveler's mecca and a tourist trap. On summer evenings and Sunday afternoons, the narrow streets of Montmartre are packed with tourists hunting for original oil paintings and a quaint café in which to eat. Few artists of any talent either live or work there now; the area is filled with hacks who imitate the style of Utrillo and Cezanne and Manet. The galleries are loaded with their products, all aimed at the tourist traffic. In half-a-dozen visits over a period of twenty years I have yet to see displayed the work of a single contemporary artist of merit.

If one visits this old quarter early in the morning, before the tourists have had a chance to get organized, one can roam the narrow, winding streets at leisure, enjoying the old stucco buildings painted in bright, lively shades of green and red and blue. Small cafés and bistros are frequented at that time by the residents of the area who are just beginning to move about and prepare for the onslaught of visitors who will start to arrive in the afternoon. The pace is leisurely; the residents are friendly.

The dingy little flat that Debussy occupied in the Rue Cardinet is in great contrast to the gaiety and color of Montmartre. Yet, behind the bleak and dirty facade, in a small apartment within this narrow building, one of the most beautiful creations of Debussy's career took seed and was

122

The entrance to Debussy's apartment on the Rue de Londre. Here his friend Stephan Mallarmé visited the composer shortly after Debussy had completed his *Prélude à l'après-midi d'un faune* based on the poet's ecologue of the same title.

Villa at St. Jean-de-Luz where the Debussys spent the composer's last summer away from Paris. Already fatally ill with cancer, the composer was discouraged at the tides of World War I.

nurtured. It was in this flat, now marked by a plaque, that *Pelléas and Mélisande* was started, a work of epic proportions which occupied the composer for ten long years.

Debussy's next residence was in Rue de Londre, a somewhat more cheerful residence, another of the Haussmann-inspired apartment buildings. Remarkable things took place here. The first was described in a letter Debussy wrote to a friend. He had just completed an orchestral work inspired by his friend Mallarmé's ecologue, *l'Après-midi d'un faune.*

> "Mallarmé has come to visit me at my little furnished flat here in the Rue de Londre. After listening to my *Prelude to the Afternoon of a Faun* he remained silent for a long time. Then he said, 'I didn't expect anything like that. The music draws out the emotion of my poem and gives it a warm background color.' "

Next, in this same furnished apartment, Debussy turned to another orchestral work. "I am creating," he said, "three *Nocturnes* for orchestra. It is an experiment with different combinations that can be obtained from one color, – like a study of gray or black in a painting."

While living on Rue de Londre, the composer met a young Parisian dressmaker who had come from one of the southern provinces of France. After a period of courtship, Debussy joyously wrote a friend, "I must tell you immediately what has happened. Lily Texier has changed her unmelodious name to Lily Debussy!"

Some troubled years for the composer followed. First there was difficulty over the first production of *Pelléas.* Debussy had hired Mary Garden to sing the leading role; the author, Maurice Maeterlinck, expected his wife to be featured as Mélisande. In anger, Maeterlinck wrote vile criticisms of the music for any newspaper that would publish them.

Finally, on April 30, 1902, the opera was performed at the Opéra-Comique. The reviews were mixed, but the Berlin paper, *Morgen,* perhaps gave the most prophetic evaluation when it said that "*Pelléas* is one of the three or four outstanding achievements in French musical history."

Marital troubles erupted next. Debussy had started seeing Emma Bardac, *née* Moyse, the wife of a wealthy financier, shortly after his marriage to Lily Texier. Several times he considered abandoning Lily for Emma. Finally, after a daughter was born to them whom they named Claude-Emma, Debussy and Mme. Bardac each filed for a divorce so that they could be married. A public scandal hit Paris when Lily Texier Debussy attempted suicide while waiting for the divorce to become final. The public and most of Debussy's friends turned against him. He then fled in desperation to Eastbourne with the partially completed score of *La Mer* — "The Sea."

EASTBOURNE AND THE BOIS DE BOULOGNE

Eastbourne is on the southern coast of England and is a typical British beach resort. Debussy called it "a little English seaside place, silly as these places sometimes are." There is a broad expanse of sandy beach, then a wide avenue. Along the northern side of this street, a series of large Victorian hotels face the ocean. From the balconies of these hotels one can watch the promenades up and down the street of the visitors, and look across the avenue to see the bathers enjoying dips in the cold waters of the Atlantic.

I was fascinated by the great contrast I found here compared to the California beach resorts which I have visited for most of my life. In Eastbourne, a man does not appear on the waterfront promenade unless he his properly dressed in suit and tie and his wife attired in a conservative dress. One goes down onto the sand itself dressed in this manner!

On the beach a very special ritual takes place. The British do not put on their bathing suits in their hotel rooms and then overdress with a suit or frock. Instead, they carry large towels which they wrap around themselves on the sand and then, under these protective covers, shimmy out of their clothes and into bathing suits. I am certain that we shocked the entire

125

waterfront populace when we went to the beach in California fashion with our swimming trunks on under our trousers. Without benefit of towel or umbrella, we simply stood on the beach and disrobed. I'll never know what the seaside crowd thought as we boldly dropped our trousers to reveal that we were already wearing bathing suits!

Our hotel was near the one which Debussy had occupied earlier in the century. His had a huge ornate front of concrete with many caryatids and highly decorated with Victorian geegaws. I already possessed a photograph of Debussy standing on the balcony of his room facing the sea with a camera in his hand to take a picture himself. He loved the sea and wrote that "the sea has shown me all her moods; she has been very good to me."

It was at Eastbourne that Debussy completed his magnificent *La Mer.*

He returned to Paris and to a financial security that he had never known before. Emma Bardac, now the second Mme. Debussy, had considerable financial resources of her own and provided funds for a home she and her husband purchased at 12 Avenue du Bois de Boulogne (now Avenue Foch), about halfway between the Arch of Triumph and the nearby Bois de Boulogne, that wonderful forest-park that lies but a mile from the heart of Paris.

We directed the taxi driver to take us to 12 Avenue Foch only to discover that the home at this address bore no resemblance to the house in some photographs I had of the former Debussy residence. I questioned several persons on the street, none of whom knew where the old Debussy home was located. Thinking that perhaps my knowledge of French was inadequate for the occasion, I had the taxi driver inquire of an elderly lady who was in the front yard of her home. Yes, she had heard that a musician had once lived in a house around the corner, but she didn't know his name and wasn't sure if it was "Debussy" or not. It seemed incredible to me that no one in the area knew where the house was in which Debussy had lived for

Debussy's home on the avenue Bois de Boulogne (now Avenue Foche), in that wonderful forest-park that lies but a mile from the heart of Paris.

Entrance to the Debussy home. Here the composer spent the last ten years of his life in virtual seclusion, since many of his friends deserted him after the attempted suicide of his first wife.

the last twelve years of his life, his only "permanent" home, the only residence he ever owned!

We followed the old lady's directions and walked around the corner and down a little side street which ended in a cul-de-sac. As we approached the end of it, I spotted the former Debussy home about the same time that the taxi driver saw a little tablet on the wall of the house announcing the spot as the old Debussy residence.

A wrought-iron fence covered with ivy surrounds the property; branches of huge poplars overhang the fence and hide most of the house behind it. I rang and rang the bell beside the iron gate. I had almost resigned myself to never seeing the building when finally the caretaker emerged from the basement and came to the gate. In my best French (which leaves much to be desired) I explained the purpose of my visit and respectfully requested permission to see the former Debussy residence. Since I seemed to be losing my case, the taxi driver pleaded it for me. The caretaker told us that the house now belonged to an American colonel who had been stationed at NATO head-quarters in Paris but who had now been transferred to Brussels. Since the colonel was not in residence, the caretaker explained that he couldn't give us permission to enter the house. "Why should you want to go into the home anyway," he asked, "since none of the Debussy furnishings remain?" But he recanted enough to allow us to enter the garden and to take photographs of the exterior.

There is a small garden in front of the home, perhaps forty feet square. A beautiful green lawn is surrounded on all four sides by a gravel pathway which is shaded by the large poplars. A small fish pond is located on the north side with two little cherubs holding fishes whose mouths spray water into the pool.

I had seen photographs of Debussy in this yard. In one he was flying a kite with his friend Louis Laloy; in others, he was playing with his daughter whom he affectionately called Chouchou. This garden hadn't changed at all from those photographs of fifty years earlier.

128

The house itself is a two-story building of sandstone with mansard roof. The gables of the attic rooms project toward the garden. The tall narrow windows are trimmed in white, while the main entrance, framed by tall Italian cypress, is a heavy double door painted a rich forest green.

What the interior of the house looked like I shall never know, for we were not admitted. Likewise, I have been unable to locate any kind of description of the rooms in any of Debussy's correspondence, or in any of the authoritative biographies of the composer.

Debussy at first enjoyed the security of his new home, but soon came to feel that he did not want to be dependent on his wife for his income. He confessed to his friend Laloy, "You know who provides the air I breathe!" He then started to make guest appearances at concert halls and opera houses to earn some money of his own. He made two trips to London and short visits to Vienna, Budapest, and Turin. He later traveled to Moscow and St. Petersburgh. On his tour to London in 1909 he learned that he had cancer. Before he left the British Isles he was resorting to cocaine and morphine. From this time on his health declined steadily.

Back at his home on Avenue du Bois de Boulogne, Debussy continued to work as best he could. He was sitting in the little front garden of his home when word reached him that fighting had broken out between Germany and France, the start of World War I. "It is almost impossible to work," he commented. "To tell the truth, one hardly dares to, for the facets of the war are more distressing than one imagines."

By 1915 his health was in a precarious state. The following summer he spent at Le Moulleau-Arcachon and the summer of 1917 at St. Jean de Luz. There he occupied a beautiful Mediterranean style house on the side of a hill overlooking the Gulf of Vizcaya. Situated among pine and cypress trees, the home is surrounded by a stucco wall in which a central wooden gate grants access to the residence. A red tile roof shows the Spanish influence in the architectural design of this low, rambling stucco home with dark oak door and deep-set windows.

He returned to his home near the Bois de Boulogne and completed his *Violin Sonata*, his last work. On May 5, 1917, he appeared on a concert platform for the last time, playing the piano part of that sonata.

The bombardment of Paris by the long range artillery of the German army began on Saturday, March 23, 1918. Debussy heard the dreadful sound of the shells exploding in the street. By this time he was too weak to be carried down the stairs to the protection of the cellar. He died on Monday, March 25, at ten in the evening.

The funeral took place in his home. Of this service, his friend Louis Laloy has written:

> "I can see as in a bad dream the coffin near the piano and the musicians in their soldier uniforms. . . . The door kept opening and closing and there was no more room for flowers. . . . The sky was overcast. There was a rumbling in the distance. Was it a storm or the explosion of a shell? Along the wide avenues there was nothing to be seen but military trucks."

By the time the procession reached the cemetery of Père-Lachaise, half of the fifty people who started from the Avenue du Bois de Boulogne had hurried to the protective walls of their own homes. Only one oration was made at the graveside as the Germans were even then invading the city.

IX
RICHARD STRAUSS: A HERO'S LIFE?

Munich, capital of Bavaria, was the birthplace of Richard Strauss. Though travels led him to three different continents, the composer always maintained his home in or near Munich. Perhaps he agreed with the American author Thomas Wolfe who wrote:

> "How can one speak of Munich except to say it is a kind of German heaven. Some people sleep and dream they are in Paradise, but all over Germany people sometimes dream that they have gone to Munich in Bavaria. And really, in an astonishing way, the city is a great Germanic dream translated into life. . . . The thing is felt in Munich more than it is seen, and for this reason, the seduction and mystery are greater." [1]

Munich is a very old city. *Marienplatz*, the main square, lies exactly where in the Middle Ages the east-west and south-north salt trade routes intersected and where wagon loads of grain changed hands. On one side of it, rising to a height of 320 feet, are the twin towers – capped by onion-shaped domes – of the Gothic cathedral which appear over the high gabled houses. On the other side the eye is caught by the spire of the Romanesque church of St. Peter's, the *alte Peter* of popular song.

Today the square is dominated by the New Town Hall (which dates from the fifteenth century). Its marble facade, darkened by the ages, rises to spires and a tower rich with intricate stone carvings. Above the pointed arch of the main entrance is the *Glockenspiel*, the clock that so fascinates children and tourists alike. Just before the noon hour, two knights and their squires come out from an alcove in the tower and move slowly around. One of them unhorses the other with

[1]Wolfe, Thomas. *Web and Rock*. New York: Harper Brothers, 1939

his lance. Then a group of red-coated barrel makers dance to the melody of an old folk song. When that is over, a cock — much higher up — flaps his wings three times, crowing shrilly over the noise of the traffic. Above this, the Queen of Heaven then dispenses her blessing on the city and its people. The four colorful genii at her feet symbolize the fight against war, famine, plague, and heresy.

But if these time-honored buildings represent the art and architecture of Munich, it is in the beer gardens that one encounters the spirit of the city. Probably the best known to the tourist is the *Hofbräuhaus* since it is located just off the *Stachus*, the busiest square in all of Germany and the center of the town. The exterior of this building is designed in the typically Bavarian style of the Renaissance, while its interior is a maze of rooms, halls, and alcoves. And in each of these, on all three floors and covering an area of a quarter city block, people are laughing, shouting, dancing, singing, talking, drinking beer, and eating. There are perhaps half a dozen bands throughout the beer hall; several are probably the old peasant Schrammel bands with members dressed in lederhosen.

More fascinating, however, since it attracts more Munchners and few tourists, is the outdoor beer garden a short distance from the *Stachus*. Festive lights overhead stretch as far as the eye can see; tables and chairs fill every inch of this vast space. In this convivial atmosphere there are perhaps more than 2000 people on a summer evening drinking large steins of beer and conversing with friends.

A holiday spirit pervades Munich for much of the year. First comes *Fasching*, the mad, carefree pre-Lenten carnival with its succession of revels, masquerades, balls, and parades. Next comes the first tapping of "March ale"; later, the first tapping of "May bock" in a ceremonial occasion. Finally comes the *Oktoberfest* with the citizens donning native costumes, gathering in huge beer tents for a drink, the children enjoying the ferris wheel and sideshow attractions.

Rathaus in Feldafing, a little hamlet buried in the hills and forests southeast of Munich, where Richard Strauss first met Pauline de Ahna.

Strauss rented this home in Marquartstein in the Bavarian Alps and composed his *Sinfonia Domestica, Also Sprach Zarathustra, Don Quixote* and his opera *Salome* in this idyllic setting.

133

This is the milieu into which Richard Strauss was born. His father was a well-known and highly respected horn player in the Munich Court Orchestra. His mother was the well-to-do daughter of the most prominent family of brewers in Bavaria, the Pschorrs.

Because of the destruction in Munich during World War II, there are almost no buildings left associated with the first years of Strauss' life. The house in which he was born, at No. 2 Altheimereck, was demolished. The Strauss apartment had occupied the second floor while the rest of the building housed the Pschorr brewery. Today a small, crudely built nightclub of the cheapest sort occupies the spot. Nothing marks it as the birthplace of Munich's famous son.

Ludwig's Gymnasium, where young Richard first attended school, was totally destroyed in 1944.. Likewise, the Royal University which he later attended, and the Odeon where he first conducted, were demolished during the war. The only place of significance left is the Bavarian State Opera House where Richard's father was employed and where the boy himself first studied music and attended concerts and opera.

The Bavarian State Opera House was first built to a design by Karl von Fischer in 1818, then known as the *Hof- und Nationaltheater.* After its destruction by fire in 1823, it was rebuilt by Leo von Klenze within two years. It was to this theater that mad King Ludwig first brought Wagner; it was in this house that Strauss heard his operas *Friedenstag* (1936) and *Capriccio* (1941) first performed.

Most of the portico and much of the interior were destroyed during the bombing raids of 1943. Restoration of the building to its original design and appearance was completed in 1964 at a cost of $15,000,000. Today the marble halls and the baroque magnificence of its auditorium attract opera lovers from all over the world. The house has five horseshoe tiers rising straight up in gleaming ranks of filigreed gold in ivory standing out against the red plush of the walls. It is an intimate theater, for there are only 2,100 seats and the last full row in the

134

orchestra is only eighteen rows from the footlights. The stage is enormous and the pit can hold a full symphony orchestra.

If the Strauss birthplace is unmarked, his name is well-known within the walls of the opera house. Each summer the Munich Festival mounts several of the composer's more popular operas.

THE TRAVELS AND TRAVAILS

In his booklet, *Recollections and Reflections*, Richard Strauss writes that an attack of pneumonia during the season of 1891 kept him from conducting at Bayreuth. "When, a year later, I had another slight attack of pleurisy, my uncle Georg Pschorr generously sent me to Egypt with 5000 Marks so that I could convalesce fully. . . . In Luxor I scored the first act of *Guntram*." [1]

[1]Strauss, Richard. *Recollections and Reflections*. London: Boosey and Hawkes, Ltd., 1949

We flew to Cairo via United Arab Airlines, a rather unique experience. I had been axious to sample Arabian cuisine and had the opportunity to do so during the flight. It convinced me that the rather pallid British cooking at our hotel in Cairo was quite delicious and palatable by comparison.

From Cairo we visited the pyramids of Ghiza and the Sphinx, monuments of and to the past that led Strauss to write that his visit to see them had changed his whole outlook on past civilizations and pre-Christian works of art. It was in Cairo that Strauss, by working up to six hours a day, completed the piano score of his first opera.

We flew on to Luxor from Cairo on *Misrair*, the intra-Egyptian airline, commonly known to European travelers as "Misery" airlines. (A flight on it proves the appropriateness of its nickname.) Our reservations had been booked at Hotel Luxor, the same old English hotel at which Strauss had stayed a half-century earlier. That old Victorian hostelry is just across

135

the street from the Temple of Luxor, through whose tall, stately columns we could see the broad Nile flowing past.

Here at Luxor, Amenhotep III, with the spoils from the victories of Thutmose III, began to build his most stately temple to Amon. Unfortunately death intervened and it was neglected for a century until Ramses II finished it in regal fashion. As Will Durant has said, "At once the quality of Egyptian architecture floods the spirit: here are scope and power, not beauty merely, but a masculine sublimity." [1]

We entered this thirty-century-old temple via a wide court now covered with sand, but once covered — before the ravages of time had taken their toll — with marble. Majestic colonnades tower on three sides; every surface is covered with hand-carved stone bas relief. Royal statues, "proud even in desolation," abound. A court of papyriform columns — eight verticle ribs tied together with five firm bands — support massive entablatures and the remains of shade-giving porticos.

From Luxor Strauss wrote a letter home outlining his systematic daily routine:

"My day's work is very simple; I get up at 8 o'clock, have a bath and breakfast: 3 eggs, tea, home-made jam; then I go for a stroll for half an hour by the Nile in the palmgrove of the hotel, and work from 10 till 1; the orchestration of the first Act goes forward slowly but surely. At 1 o'clock I have lunch, then read my Schopenhauer or play Bezique with Mrs. Conze for a piastre stake. From 3 till 4 I work on; at 4 o'clock tea, and after that I go for a walk until 6 when I do my duty admiring the unusual sunset. At 6 o'clock it gets cool and dark; then I write letters or work a bit more until 7. At 7 dinner, after which I chat and smoke (8 to 12 a day), at half past 9 I go to my room, read for half an hour and put out the light at ten. So it goes on day after day. . . . I shall

[1]Durant, Will. *The Story of Civilization* (Volume 1) New York: Simon and Schuster, 1954

Strauss built his own villa at Garmisch-Partenkirchen in 1908, largely with the money he earned from writing *Salome*.

The entrance hall to the villa is a hodge-podge of bric-a-brac, pictures, paintings, portraits and memorabilia acquired during many conducting tours throughout Europe and America.

stay at Luxor until the middle of March. I hope I shall finish the instrumentation of Act I here." [1]

Another relic of ancient Egypt is but a short distance away, another monument that fascinated Strauss, the Temples of Karnak. It took half a hundred Pharaohs many centuries to build them for they cover sixty acres with "the lordliest offerings that architecture ever made to the gods." A broad avenue lined on either side by Sphinxes leads to the place where Champollion, founder of Egyptology, stood in 1828 and wrote:

> "I went at last to the palace, or rather the city of monuments – to Karnak. There all the magnificence of the Pharaohs appeared to me, all that men had imagined and executed on the grandest scale. . . . No people, ancient or modern, has conceived the art of architecture on a scale so sublime, so great, so grandiose, as the ancient Egyptians. They conceived like men a hundred feet high." [1]

After Strauss returned to Germany, he supervised the first production of *Guntram* at the Hoftheater in Weimar. During the rehearsal the star – Pauline de Ahna – made some kind of mistake, and; when corrected by the young Strauss who was conducting and with whom she had worked for eight years, she threw the vocal score from the stage at his head. She also shrieked and yelled insults, then ran for her dressing room.

What followed next is related by Lotte Lehmann in the words with which Strauss himself told her the story:

> "Strauss, terribly annoyed, laid down his baton, interrupted the rehearsal which had been so violently disturbed, and, without knocking, entered Pauline's artist's room. Those outside heard through the closed door wild shrieks of rage and fragmentary insults – then all was quiet. Turning pale each looked at the other; who had killed whom? A delegation of orchestra members approached the threatening door.

[1]Del Mar, Norman. *Richard Strauss* (Volume 1) New York: The Free Press of Glencoe, 1962

[2]Capart, Jean. *Thebes*. London, 1926

A shy knocking. . . . Strauss opened the door and stood in the doorway beaming. The representative of the musicians stammered his speech: 'The orchestra is so horrified by the incredibly shocking behaviour of Fraulein Pauline de Ahna that they feel they owe it to their honored conductor Strauss to refuse in the future to play in any opera in which she might have a part. . . . ' Strauss regarded the musicians smilingly. Then he said: That hurts me very much, for I have just become engaged to Fraulein de Ahna.' " [1]

After they were married, Strauss accepted a position as conductor of the Berlin Philharmonic Orchestra in addition to his regular post as Court Conductor in Munich. This was to be a long association with the Berlin orchestra, lasting from 1894 until the close of the 1918 season. (He was similarly associated with the Berlin Court Opera from 1898 until 1924.)

Of his Berlin residences, only one escaped wartime destruction. The apartment in which he lived at Kaiserdamm 39, now renamed and renumbered Heerstrasse 2, still exists in its former style. It is an unpretentious building of dark gray stucco, nondescript architecture, and some five stories tall. Most of its moderate-size apartments have a small balcony which overlooks the busy thoroughfare below.

During World War I Strauss took up residence in neutral Switzerland; during World War II Strauss again went to Switzerland, this time after his falling-out with Hitler late in the war. On his first visit he rented a home on Mythenstrasse in Zurich; during the second war the composer lived at the Hotel Verenahof in Baden.

The earlier home in Zurich is gone now, for it was on the northern shore of the lake, and a broad and beautiful park has since been built between the lake and Mythenstrasse, thus causing all the homes on the lakeside of the street to be razed.

Baden, as its name implies, is a health spa with natural warm mineral water springs. This quaint town is located on some rolling hills with magnificent views from almost any spot of the

[1]Lehmann, Lotte. *My Many Lives*. New York: Boosey and Hawkes, Inc., 1948

139

rugged, more distant mountains. The narrow streets wander up and down the hillside among small, modest homes and a great number of hotels. The Verenahof in which Richard and Pauline Strauss sat out the war is one of the few hotels that border on the mineral wells themselves. This permits the hotel guests to take the elevator from their floor to the basement and then proceed by an underground tunnel directly to the baths.

Cheerful flower boxes of petunias, asters and geraniums are to be found around the small hotel, and its front gardens are a solid dash of vivid color. The Strausses could not have helped being happy here, for it is so peaceful and quiet, yet charming in an old-fashioned way.

THE RESIDENCES

South of Munich the roads stretch back into the Isar Valley, the lakes of the plateau on either side and the Bavarian Alps, Germany's highest mountains, on the horizon. For about 180 miles the wooded ridges and jagged peaks of the Alps form the frontier with Switzerland, sentinels with names like Mädelegabel, Grosser Daumen, Zugspitze, Harzogstand, and Utersberg. The entire plateau leading to these majestic peaks is strewn with little churches with onion-shaped towers set in a patchwork of field and forest. Bavarian houses of wood and stucco, each with bright-colored flower boxes on their balconies, nestle on the side of the rolling hills.

The little village of Marquartstein lies about eight miles south of Chiemsee (known locally as "The Bavarian Sea") and fifty miles east of Munich. Even today the town is well off the beaten path. The road leads leisurely south off the Autobahn and into some rolling foothills. As we rounded a curve, Marquartstein came into view. A small stream, whose origin is high in the Alps, runs through the village. There are perhaps less than 100 homes and shops in Marquartstein, but each is distinctive in design, yet all reflect that unique Bavarian style which combines a stuccoed exterior with wooden battens and

140

Strauss' desk in his study looks out the window toward his garden. On the desk is a photographic portrait of his wife and an assortment of pens, pen-holders and scores.

Strauss' inlaid piano was built especially for this room so that the instrument would blend with the wood paneling in the wainscotting and bookshelves.

deep-pitched roof of hand-hewn shingles. Balconies are a must, and each home seems to vie with the next to see which will have the brightest profusion of blooming geraniums in the flower boxes on the balcony. The shops are old and quaint. There is no place here for neon signs or billboards. The traditional craftsmen symbols used since the Middle Ages, cast in wrought iron, announce to the public the nature of each shop.

Past the heart of town, on a road leading further back into the mountains, stands the house in which Strauss lived while working on *Ein Heldenleben* — "A Hero's Life" — and *Salome*. Today a little plaque in the wall that surrounds the estate testifies to this fact.

The two-storied home is not large, perhaps six or seven rooms. Its white stucco exterior contrasts with the natural wood balcony in front and the ornately carved eaves. Situated on the side of a little knoll, the house is surrounded by large shade trees. A front lawn, possibly fifty feet square, wanders down the hillside. Behind the home a space has been leveled for a little patio which is surrounded by the colorful blossoms of countless varieties of flowers. Paths lead off in several directions: across a verdant meadow with stands of tall grass; back into the rugged mountains; and down the hill into the village itself.

Once Strauss had achieved a modicum of success and his compositions had earned him sufficient income, he purchased some property in Garmisch and had his own Villa constructed. He moved into this home in 1908 and lived there with his wife and only son the rest of his life, some forty-one years.

Through a mutual friend, I had been introduced (via correspondence) to Dr. Franz Strauss, the composer's son, who still lives at the Villa. We had written ahead to see if we might visit with Dr. Strauss and his charming wife and take some photographs, both of the home and of the composer's study. Dr. Strauss wrote back, saying, "So far as I understand from your cordial letter, I welcome the idea."

Garmisch lies about ninety miles due south of Munich and is

142

only five miles from the Swiss border. It hugs the foot of the Zugspitze, Germany's highest mountain peak, a health resort where the winter Olympics have been held.

The drive to Garmisch was a lengthy one, for the road climbed steeply most of the way, had countless curves and bends, and was crowded with Bavarian tourists in their camper-buses and Volkswagens, heading back into the hills for a summer's holiday.

Garmisch itself is a resort town of considerable size. The downtown area was packed with people, and its modern buildings were obviously styled in the Alpine tradition to try and impress the tourists. We were sadly disappointed in it, for it was all so contrived, all so typical of commercial enterprise.

We drove through the town and on into the suburbs, looking for No. 42 Zoepritzstrasse. It was a bright, sunny day and the leaves of the trees shimmered in the breeze that was gently blowing. We finally reached our destination.

The Villa is located on a large tract of land, perhaps an acre in size. A vast lawn stretches down to the entrance gate. Behind the Villa there is another patch of lawn, one which leads up to the trees that surround the estate. Through the trees several paths lead immediately up the rugged slope of the mountain directly behind the Villa.

I had seen many photographs of the Strauss home and had always thought its exterior design strange and ugly. I was pleasantly surprised when I saw it in its Alpine setting, for it seemed uniquely appropriate. Essentially the two-storied house of beige-colored stucco is square in shape with a hip roof of red tile. A hexagonal tower breaks into the southwest corner of the structure; a sort of onion-shaped roof surmounts it.

After wandering slowly through the gardens, enjoying the statuary and the ponds, we rang the bell at the front door and were admitted by the maid. I presented my calling card and we were asked to wait in the entrance hall. It was unbelievable! Rectangular in shape, this high-ceilinged vestibule has a spiral staircase leading to the second floor sleeping rooms. Every inch

143

of wall space of all four walls was covered with small pictures, perhaps a hundred altogether. Some were artistic oil paintings, some were portraits, some photographs, some religious articles. Gaudy rococo frames of gold hung alongside ultra-modern frames of the 1930's. A beautiful Chinese vase, some three feet tall, stood by the newel post of the stairway. Two Biedermeier chests with marble tops stood in the hallway, one on either side.

Finally the Strausses descended the stairway to greet us. Frau Alice spoke excellent English and thought that perhaps she could be a better guide for us than Dr. Franz, who spoke no English. He then excused himself after giving us a hearty welcome in the Bavarian dialect.

There are fifteen rooms in the house; the servants' quarters are over the garage to the rear of the estate. Three rooms of Richard Strauss remain as he left them: his studio, his library, and his parlor. The other downstairs rooms are used daily by Franz and Alice Strauss: a dining room, a sitting room, another parlor, a breakfast room, and the cooking area. The bedrooms, sewing room, and other sitting rooms are upstairs.

We first went into the composer's study. The room is large. The master's grand piano stands to the right side. The case was especially constructed for this room and finished in light fruitwood to match the wainscoating of the walls. A very large desk, of matching wood, stands nearby. An inkwell, books, small statues, papers and a lamp fill the top of the desk except for a working area in the center. Across the room, opposite the piano, are some overstuffed chairs and a couch. Over the sofa is the original oil painting by W. V. Krausz of Strauss conducting an orchestra. To the side of the room is a fine etching of the composer by Max Liebermann. It was undoubtedly in this room that Strauss entertained Hugo von Hofmannsthal while collaborating with him on *Elektra, Rosenkavalier, Ariadne auf Naxos, Die Frau ohne Schatten, Die Aegyptische Helena, Arabella,* and *Die Liebe der Danae.*

There is a small anteroom between the master's study and the parlor. The walls are lined with glass-doored bookcases of

144

The patio of the villa at Garmisch shows off the colorful flower
beds which were a particular delight of the composer. He could
enjoy long walks in the forest behind his home and spend his
social hours visiting with friends in the patio.

View of Baden from the railway station, the Swiss health resort to
which the Strausses came during the closing years of World War II.

gray-painted wood. Some are filled with books; in others, statuary, manuscripts, citations, and various awards bestowed on the composer are displayed. The room is lighted by a small chandelier of rock crystal, and there is a small desk which Strauss used for correspondence. A fine alabaster bust of Richard Strauss by Hugo Lederer stands on a pedestal in the corner. One of the most fascinating things in the room is the manuscript of the *Schneider Polka* which is on display in one of the breakfronts. This was Richard Strauss' first composition, written in 1871 when he was seven years old. The composer himself had considered the manuscript irretrivably lost, but several years ago his son, Franz Strauss, came across it at an auction, purchased it, and placed it on display here!

The adjoining parlor is filled with furniture that Strauss rescued from his Vienna home during World War II. The overstuffed chairs and divan are covered in a rich maroon fabric, while a fine tapestry hangs on the wall above the couch. On the opposite side of the room are some of Strauss' valuable oils, painted by such masters as El Greco, Tintoretto, and Rubens. This is a quiet room, an intimate room, yet actually spacious and impressive.

Richard Strauss and his beloved wife Pauline lived at Garmisch for many happy years together. Pauline became, over the years, a very strong-willed woman who carefully guarded her famous husband from curiosity seekers and opportunists. (Strauss often said that of his operas, his favorite was *Intermezzo* — the story of a musician and his termagant wife!) When, after a long and fruitful life as a composer and conductor, Richard Strauss passed away at Garmisch on September 8, 1949, Pauline only oulived him by eight months.

X
RAVEL: A PERSONIFICATION OF THE FRENCH SOUL

Just north of the Spanish border the French seacoast makes a gentle curve inland forming a crescent-shaped bay, the *Baie de St. Jean de Luz*. It is cradled in the foothills of the Pyrenees and dominated by the nearby *la Rhûne* which towers to a majestic height of 3000 feet. A little river, the Nivelle, wanders through these mountains and then flows into the bay at its midpoint.

A town has grown up around the bay on both sides of the river, actually two sister cities. On the south side of the Nivelle is Ciboure, a village of 5000 inhabitants; to the north is St. Jean de Luz, a town of 11,000 residents. The width of the river separates these two municipalities that are joined by a single bridge. St. Jean de Luz is the better known, especially as a pleasure resort, but it was in Ciboure that Maurice Ravel was born on March 7, 1875.

This is Basque country, a land of fishermen. Today bright sails and tall masts of fishing boats rock slowly back and forth as the craft ply the waters or enter the small harbor, the *Porte de pêche*, that has been built where the river broadens a bit. Fish nets, hung out to dry, drape gracefully from posts on the bank. Baskets of fish stand side by side on the shore as hearty fishermen unload their catch for the day. Larger boats bring in tuna for which this area is noted. The scene is colorful; the pace is leisurely.

We arrived from Paris by train and immediately caught a taxi for l'Hôtel Edouard VII, a wonderful hostelry operated by the Simpsons, a fine old family of British origin. By the time we checked in, it was about 11 a.m., so we decided to change into our swimming clothes and enjoy the beach before pursuing our Ravel pilgrimage. The day was bright and sunny; there wasn't a cloud in the sky. We discovered a fine sandy beach sheltered from the wind and temperate water for swimming. Bathing

147

tents and umbrellas of bright red and orange and yellow dotted the *plage* and reminded me of photographs I had seen of Ravel in later life enjoying a Sunday picnic on the sand at this very spot.

Suddenly we noticed that everyone seemed to be leaving the beach. They were packing up their tents and umbrellas, gathering up their blankets and beach towels, loading children's toys and beach balls into large hampers. At first, the only reason for this of which we could think was that it was twelve noon and perhaps the bathers were observing the lunch hour as shop-keepers do by shutting up their establishments and going home for an hour. But surely, with food and drink stands along the quay, and with picnic baskets readily available to bring one's own lunch, there would be no reason to go to all the trouble of packing up all belongings and trekking them back to a car or cottage for an hour!

At one o'clock our suspicions were confirmed. The same people emerged and started setting up the same tents and umbrellas on the beach; they laid out the same towels and blankets. The lunch-time *siesta* was over!

St. Jean de Luz is the ancient land of the Basques. That evening we enjoyed watching some of the townsfolk perform dances in native costumes on the green in the village square. Young people danced a fast and lively *fandango*, while later some of the older folk did the Dance of Arçeaux, or, in Basque, *Arku Dantza*. The setting was impressive, for the Château Lohobiague-Haraneder formed the background. This is the two-storied stone house in which Louis XIV stayed in 1660 before his marriage the following day to Marie-Thérèse of Spain in the nearby fourteenth-century Church of *St. Jean Baptiste*.

Although as an infant Maurice Ravel lived here only three months, he returned as a youth many times for extended holidays, and, as an adult, usually spent long vacations here. Surely the music, the songs, the customs of these Basques influenced him. His first notable work, *Pavane pour une Infante défunte* – the "Pavane for a Dead Princess" – shows traces of

The French fishing village of Ciboure on the Basque coast just seven miles from the Spanish border. In 1874 Joseph Ravel returned from a business trip to Spain with his bride from New Castile, and settled here.

The Ravel home in Ciboure had been built centuries earlier by a Dutch pirate. Maurice Ravel was born in this house on March 7, 1875.

his Basque origin. "The whole *raison d'être* of the work," says Norman Demuth in his biography of Ravel, "is the stately pavane danced in front of the bier of a Spanish princess which dance was a characteristic one of old Spain."[1] Later works similarly showed the Spanish-Basque influence of this seaside resort. Consider *Une Barque sur l'océan* (1905), the *Rapsodie espagnole* with its "Prélude à la Nuit," "Malagueña," "Habanera" and "Feria" (1907), the *Chanson espagnole* (1910), and, certainly, his most famous work, the *Bolero* (1928).

Early the next morning we started out in search of the house in which Ravel was born. Our hotel was on the north side of the bay, so we walked along the quay as we headed for Ciboure on the other side of the river. While some of the beachfront homes were of a later period, many of the old structures were of the peculiar style developed by the Basques with deeply carved eaves, wooden balconies with intricately sculptured railings, and walls of stucco with wooden battens running throughout.

We crossed the bridge to Ciboure by the *Porte de pêche* and continued along the waterfront street, now known as *Quai Maurice Ravel*, to Number 12. (At the time of the composer's birth it was called *Quai de la Nivelle*.) The old Ravel home stood out in stark contrast to the adjoining waterfront houses. The others were all of Basque design with tiled roofs; number 12 looked as through it was of Flemish design — a tall, somewhat narrow building with its roof hidden by the curving swirls of the uppermost portion of the facade (see the illustration). Iron instead of wooden shutters protected its windows; its balcony railings were of wrought iron, not of wood. The entire front was of stone and stucco; none of the ornate wood carving of the Basques was to be seen.

Back at our hotel we asked Miss Jeannine Simpson, the daughter of our host, the reason for the incongruity in the design of the Ravel home. She told us an interesting story. It seems that back in the early days of this area, Dutch pirates roamed up and down the Atlantic seacoasts of France, Spain,

[1]Demuth, Norman. *Ravel*. London: J. M. Dent and Sons, Ltd., 1947

and Portugal, capturing and plundering many boats. As they became rich from their bounty, some of them wished to settle down, at least temporarily. Because they were exiles from their native Netherlands, some chose the little known port of Ciboure/St. Jean de Luz, hidden as it is near the French-Spanish border, in which to build their homes. Either out of homesickness or because they knew no other style, they had their houses built in the old Flemish medieval style. The Ravel home was a remnant of some early Dutch pirate's desire to settle down.

ON TO PARIS

We caught the night train from St. Jean de Luz for Paris to continue on with our pilgrimage.

The Ravels established themselves first at 40 Rue de Martyr when they moved to Paris. This is an old apartment building with lacy wrought-iron railings around its balconies. Here their second son, Edouard, was born. Although their apartment was sparsely furnished, the family never felt privation.

They next moved to 73 Rue Pigalle, another of the Hausmann-inspired Parisian apartment buildings. The Ravels occupied a flat on the top floor. This gave young Maurice a splendid opportunity to pursue his hobby of astronomy, for he could get an excellent view of the sky from their sixth-floor balcony. When the lad tired of this, he would go indoors and, by the light of a green-shaded oil lamp, practise tricks of magic or build a house from a box of matches. (The boy was both full of mischief and high spirits according to his friends.)

Years later, after Ravel had finished his studies at the Conservatory, he went one evening to the Opéra-Comique with some of his artist friends. As they were wending their way through the crowd, they accidentally bumped into a paperboy who exclaimed as he was hit, "Look out for the Apaches!" From this moment on, this group of artists called themselves *The Apaches.*

At first they met in the home of one of its members on the

151

Rue de Long, a typical Hausmann-designed street filled with apartment buildings of complementary styles. Their secret call was a theme from Borodin's *Symphony No. 2* which they whistled.

A little later the Apaches changed their meeting place to a home in Auteil, a little suburb a short ride from Paris, a much more secluded location for their *rendezvous*. Here the homes and apartment houses are not so crowded; small gardens with shrubs, flowers, and trees can be found in front of some of the stone and brick buildings. "We would meet in Auteil," said one of the Apaches, "and read or play whatever we had recently written or composed. We had, more or less, the same tastes in art which was lucky for people as hot-headed as we were!" This circle of Apaches included, at one time or another, Cocteau, Gide, Diaghilev, Nijinsky, and such musicians as Florent Schmitt and Manuel de Falla. One of the last to join was Igor Stravinsky, a refugee from Russia.

In 1908, after his father passed away, Ravel and his mother moved into an apartment with his brother Edouard on Avenue Carnot. From the windows of their flat they could see the majestic Arch of Triumph which was but a block away. Standing on their balcony they could see the traffic move around this monument in a mass of concentric circles. One of the composer's first visitors to this apartment was Serge Diaghilev, the ballet impresario, who had come to ask Ravel to write a ballet score based on the old Greek legend of Daphnis and Chloe.

MONTFORT L'AMAURY

In 1920 Maurice Ravel purchased a home of his own in Montfort l'Amaury, a small village about an hour's drive from Paris. Although it was a small home of hardly more than half a dozen rooms, he gave it the grandiose name of "Le Belvédère."

The road through Montfort l'Amaury makes a wide curve around a hillside as it leads out of town. Trees and wild patches of berries cover the slope above the road; on the downhill side,

Le Belvédère in the quiet village of Montfort–l'Amaury, only thirty miles from Paris, was Ravel's own "villa." It was so tiny that his friends called it the "doll's house."

The bedroom had Greek columns painted on the wall by the composer; part of a canopied, Directoire-style bed can be seen to the right.

right on the street's edge, stands Le Belvédère. Built of red brick, the window frames, the wooden shutters, and the door jambs are painted white. A small, square tower occupies the center position of the street facade; a red slate roof completes the picture. Although the home appears to be a single story dwelling, there are rooms on a lower level in back made possible by the slope of the hill. A garden with a central fish pond leads further on down the hillside.

Ravel delighted in furnishing and decorating this home, and it remains today just as he left it in 1937; even his eyeglasses still rest on his desk.

Some of the *objets d'art* are beautiful and genuine; others are cheap imitations with which he used to embarrass his guests. He would show his friends some Japanese or Chinese ornaments, and, when they had expressed "oohs" and "ahs" at the exquisite loveliness of them, he would inform them that the ornaments were cheap fakes. Sometimes he would point to a glass bowl; when similar cries of delight were made, he would remark that it was only a glass bowl for an electric ceiling light! Perhaps it was that he detested the *snobisme* so prevalent in his day and he rebelled against it, for he had already rebelled against the then current notion that "artists" must necessarily be unkempt, dirty, and *outré* in appearance. He always dressed in an ultra-smart, double-breasted suit with matching or complementary tie. Gone was the beard of his youth; his silver-grey hair was always well groomed.

We had telephoned ahead to make arrangements for visiting Le Belvédère. When we arrived we were greeted at the door by the very charming Mme. Céleste Albaret who now lives at Le Belvédère as housekeeper and curator. She was a fascinating person to meet as she had been Marcel Proust's housekeeper for the last years of his life. (In *Proust*, George Painter wrote, ". . . she lived with him, fed, nursed and comforted him, taking the place of the young mother of his infancy.") She had been the model of "beautiful Françoise," the housekeeper in Proust's masterpiece, *Remembrance of Things Past*.

The parlor was small, but furnishing it became an absorbing occupation for the composer. Its minuscule proportions satisfied his love for small and pretty things, and challenged his talent for creating beauty within a limited capacity.

The crowded study was painted black, and Ravel's piano dominated the small room. Over it hung the portrait of the composer's mother.

Mme. Albaret was most patient with my faltering French (she speaks no English) and claimed she could understand me completely. She led us first to Ravel's studio, a smallish room whose walls he painted a somber black above the imitation green marble wainscoating! A single window let light shine across the master's desk, still covered by his acquisitions of many years – an embossed leather music portfolio, an ornate brass pencil holder, a fancy pipe rack, a knickknack bowl of pewter, a lacquered box, his glasses, and, most important, ash trays. (Ravel was an inveterate smoker from earliest youth; he even refused to make a concert tour of America unless he could be supplied with more than the legal quota of his favorite French Gauloise cigarettes while here.)

On the wall above his desk hang two oil portraits, one of Maurice at age six and one of his brother Edouard at eight. On the opposite side of the room is the composer's piano. Its top is covered with bibelot: a three-masted sailing ship carved out of ivory mounted in a bell jar with sea shells surrounding it; a tiny mechanical feathered bird in a brass cage that flits it wings and chirps when the key in the base is wound; a peacock candle-holder in the *art nouveau* style; a large, overly ornate brass and marble pedestal of classic Victorian design; and an assortment of pictures and small souvenirs in addition to electric lamps in the style of turn-of-the-century brass chimney lamps.

We asked if we might see his sitting room, the one decorated in Oriental style about which I had read so much. It was in this room that we found the authentic beside the cheap copy, the beautiful *objet d'art* beside a piece of trivia! Chinoiseries fascinated Ravel; this was evident from the glass Oriental wind-chime that hung on the door (in an inoperative position) as we entered the room. The composer made no attempt to imitate Oriental furniture, but breakfronts in the room display an assortment of imported China plates, carved figures (were any of them authentic?), while a Japanese tea set rested on the "coffee" table in front of the chesterfield.

156

In the small dining room, Mme. Albaret showed us chairs of a pseudo-Greek design which Ravel had painted himself. He had painted the chairs black (what *was* his obsession with this color?); on the backs of them he had sketched figures similar to those found on ancient Greek vases and vessels in the museums – flute players, fauns and other Greek legendary characters. A small table is in the center of the room, and on the wall is his imitation Monticelli oil of which he was so proud.

Mme. Albaret led us downstairs to see Ravel's dressing room and bedroom. Both are relatively small with low ceilings. The walls of the bedroom are covered with beige wallpaper which Ravel applied to the doors also so that they tend to become part of the wall. At regular intervals, the composer painted classical Greek pilasters on the paper in black paint. Two matching arm chairs sit on either side of the fireplace over which hangs a small mirror and a landscape in oil. The bed on the side of the room is not large, but draws attention to itself by the draped canopy above it.

The walls of the sitting room are painted a cocoa brown, the doors white with black trim outlining their panels. A chaise lounge is covered in white damask with black piping. Shelves to the side of the room contain more Oriental vases, cups, and pots. A Japanese sake set and lacquered tray rest on the hassock in front of an oval mirror. The table beside the arm chair is cluttered with countless objects, souvenirs of Ravel's many trips.

From the sleeping quarters we wandered out into the garden, for they are on the same level because of the slope of the hill. The garden, like the house, is in miniature. Ravel loved to garden and spent many hours planting flowers and tending to them as they grew. We found an all-white cat sitting contentedly on the grass watching the fish pond with a wary eye. Mme. Albaret reminded us that when Ravel was alive, his constant companion at Le Belvédère was his white cat *Mouni*. The composer had had a constant battle trying to maintain goldfish in his pond, for Mouni became quite a fisherman!

Reluctantly we said goodbye to our hostess and headed back for Paris. It was a sad occasion, for Le Belvédère had painted such a vivid picture for us of Ravel as a composer and active man; now we were going to the hospital in Paris where he spent his last days.

While swimming in the ocean at St. Jean de Luz one summer day, Ravel became aware that he no longer commanded full control over his arms and legs. Gradually this numbing effect prevented him from writing or even signing his name. While his mind remained most alert and active, his body was refusing to act and respond. Eventually his brother decided that an operation was necessary to relieve the pressure on his brain.

The hospital was the *Centre Française du Medecin,* located in the Auteuil section of Paris. The *Centre* is a U-shaped building of two stories with Mansard roof; there is a beautiful garden with large shade trees in the central courtyard. Here Ravel was operated on during the morning hours of December 9, 1937. His friend, Rolland-Manuel, has written:

> "I can still see Ravel, heroic to the bitter end, with a turban of white bandage, on the evening before the operation, laughing at the unsuspected likeness we thought he showed to Lawrence of Arabia.

> "The operation left him in a state of semi-consciousness which lasted a whole week. On Monday the 27th his life drew quietly to its end and he died without suffering in the small hours of the 28th of December."[1]

Ravel was buried in the family plot in Levallois, alongside his beloved parents. His brother Edouard eventually occupied the space next to Maurice. Like most European cemeteries, Levallois is kept in immaculate order, but the individual plots are as close to one another as they can be; space to bury the dead is at a premium.

[1]Roland-Manuel. *A la gloire de Ravel.* Paris: Editions de la Nouvelle Revue Critique, 1938.

158

The balconeyed apartment on the Rue des Martyr in Paris where Joseph Ravel, his wife and infant son Maurice first lived. Here the Ravels' second son, Edouard, was born.

The entrance to the home of Maurice and Edouard Ravel which they shared after the death of their father. It was through this doorway that Nijinsky entered to discuss the production of *Daphnis et Chloé*.

After viewing the tombstone with its little bouquet of red geraniums, we wandered outside the confines of the cemetery only to find a playground on the other side of the wall. This small playground is dedicated to Maurice Ravel whose sculptured portrait rests in the wall beside the entrance. What a wonderful tribute to the gentle composer who so loved children that he wrote for them *The Mother Goose Suite.*

At the dedication of this playground, a friend spoke knowingly of the composer:

> "Maurice Ravel was one of the most noble personifications of the French soul. Elegant in his simplicity, disdainful of appearances, faithful in his friendships, indulgent to ingratitude, capable of all delicacy and also of all audacity, he inspired the beginning of this century with his radiance."

Our pilgrimage had come to its close.